REINVENTING
REFERENCE

REINVENTING REFERENCE

How libraries deliver value in the age of Google

Edited by **Katie Elson Anderson** and **Vibiana Bowman Cvetkovic**

An imprint of the American Library Association

CHICAGO 2015

Katie Elson Anderson is a reference and instruction librarian at the Paul Robeson Library, Rutgers University, Camden, New Jersey, and the coeditor of *Stop Plagiarism: A Guide to Understanding and Prevention*. Publications include chapters in *Teaching Generation M: A Handbook for Librarians and Educators*, Sage's *21st Century Anthropology: A Reference Handbook*, and *Portrayals of Children in Popular Culture, A Handbook*.

Vibiana Bowman Cvetkovic is reference librarian and web administrator at the Paul Robeson Library, Rutgers University, Camden, New Jersey. Her other books include *Stop Plagiarism: A Guide to Understanding and Prevention* and *Scholarly Resources for Children and Childhood Studies: A Research Guide and Annotated Bibliography*. She has also published in various refereed journals and library and information science publications. In 2005 she was named a *Library Journal* Mover & Shaker.

© 2015 by the American Library Association

Printed in the United States of America
19 18 17 16 15   5 4 3 2 1

ISBNs
978-0-8389-1278-2 (paper)
978-0-8389-1285-0 (PDF)
978-0-8389-1286-7 (ePub)
978-0-8389-1287-4 (Kindle)

Library of Congress Cataloging-in-Publication Data

Reinventing reference : how libraries deliver value in the age of Google / edited by Katie Elson Anderson and Vibiana Bowman Cvetkovic.
      pages   cm
   Includes bibliographical references and index.
   ISBN 978-0-8389-1278-2 (print : alk. paper)—ISBN 978-0-8389-1286-7 (epub)—
   ISBN 978-0-8389-1285-0 (pdf)—ISBN 978-0-8389-1287-4 (kindle)
   1. Reference services (Libraries) 2. Electronic reference services (Libraries) 3. Reference services (Libraries)—
Information technology. 4. Reference librarians—Effect of technological innovations on. 5. Librarians—
Professional ethics. 6. Libraries and the Internet. I. Anderson, Katie Elson, 1973–editor. II. Cvetkovic, Vibiana
Bowman, 1953–editor.
Z711.R47 2015
025.5'2—dc23   2014031542

Cover design by Kimberly Thornton. Images © Shutterstock, Inc.
Text design by Alejandra Diaz in the Benton Sans and Arno Pro typefaces.

♾ This paper meets the requirements of ANSI/NISO Z39.48-1992 (Permanence of Paper).

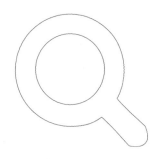

CONTENTS

PART III   "DUDE, WHERE'S MY JETPACK?" Near Future of Reference

INTRODUCTION

Referencing the Future

Katie Elson Anderson and **Vibiana Bowman Cvetkovic**

A survey of recent articles in library journals underscores an unsettling trend. Cities and towns across the United States are curtailing library hours, services, and (all too often) closing the doors. Public libraries in Pittsburgh, Philadelphia, Camden (New Jersey), Charlotte (North Carolina), and Boston have all cut services or closed branches. Public, school, and academic libraries have to deal with shrinking budgets, increasing numbers of students, and decreasing numbers of employees. Many library schools, the institutions whose charge it is to prepare the next generation of professionals, are also facing hard times. Some library schools are broadening their focus. The School of Communication, Information and Library Studies at Rutgers University, for example, is now the School of Communication and Information. Others, like the libraries themselves, are closing their doors and shutting off the lights. However, the profession is not ready to put itself on the endangered species list. Scholars, administrators, and practitioners from all aspects of librarianship are reimagining the profession as well as how information services can be delivered. The goal of this book is to contribute to that effort.

Reinventing Reference takes a critical look at the megatrends and factors (such as public policy, economics, and popular culture) that affect current library policy and practice regarding the process of delivering information services and that will continue to affect them into the foreseeable future. The contributors to this work, which include library leaders and visionaries, place these issues in historical and cultural contexts and offer practical solutions for new paradigms of reference service for all users. They also project how library services will be reshaped by new and emerging technologies.

Reinventing an Image and a Profession

The chapters in this book focus on how different libraries are adapting to the social, cultural, and technological changes that are constantly being presented to them. Librarians and educators address these changes in different ways, providing a variety of perspectives based on their research, experience, and workplace environment. These different experiences and perspectives help to provide the reader with the tools and information to move forward into the future of reference. The diverse librarian voices represented in this book are just a small sample of professionals who embrace reference librarianship in this changing and challenging time.

This is both an exciting and uncertain time to be a reference librarian. As a whole, the profession seeks to march forward with technology while not losing sight of convention and the principles reference professionals hold dear. Some chapters in this book focus on the current state of reference, detailing the challenges faced by reference librarians in academic, school, public, and special libraries as they forge ahead into the future. Other chapters look to the future to ascertain what the state of reference librarianship will be in years to come. Any discussion of the current and future states of reference should include a brief examination of the image of the reference librarian in popular culture because it is this perception of the profession by the general public that can either help or hinder a reference librarian's ability to provide services to patrons in any type of library.

The image of the librarian in popular culture has been examined, discussed, argued, mourned, and praised. Academic articles, conference presentations, books, blogs, and social media sites address the stereotypes and images of the library profession in popular culture. Much of the discussion involves how librarians are depicted in popular movies, television shows, and print and how this may affect the profession. It is difficult to make it through library school without someone referencing the movies *Desk Set* or *Party Girl*, quintessential viewing for librarians in training. If those movies are not enough, there is an annotated filmography (Raish 2011) that, while no longer being updated, is still the most complete listing of librarian appearances on the big screen. Many of the movies on the list, as well as television shows and other media, perpetuate the popular images of a librarian: female, introverted, sexy in an intellectual sort of way. Male librarians, when actually depicted, tend to be characterized as gruff, overzealous protectors of libraries and the books they contain.

It is unfortunate that many of the images of libraries and librarians in popular culture are not entirely positive, especially when the target is a younger audience. Future library patrons and supporters are being exposed to the perpetual image of the library as a dark and foreboding place of knowledge with intimidating librarian guardians. The librarian in the popular Harry Potter movies and book series, Irma Pince, is protective and possessive of the books in the library and is described by the books' own fans on the Harry Potter Wiki (2012) as "a severe and strict woman . . . thin, irritable and looked like an underfed vulture. As such, she was deemed highly unpleasant by most of the student body." The continuance of the image of the librarian as protector of books is also present in fantasy writer Terry Pratchett's popular Discworld series, whose librarian is an orangutan who was once human but prefers to remain in primate form so as to better terrify library patrons. He protects his library and the viscous, hairy books with teeth, which are tethered on chains in a rather menacing way. Another popular book among young students is *How to Train Your Dragon*, which has the horrific "Hairy-Scary Librarian," who is exactly as he is described. The main characters dare venture into the dark and dangerous library only to be violently attacked by the librarian, who does not want his books disturbed. A review of librarian stereotypes in young adult literature finds that "overall the librarians in the young adult books reviewed were portrayed in a more negative or neutral light" (Peresie and Alexander 2005, 29).

With a few exceptions, movies, television, and literature do not take advantage of the opportunity to portray librarians in a more positive light. Sadly, even the Jedi librarian in the popular series Star Wars, whose target audience includes just about everyone, portrays a stereotypical bun-wearing woman who is "superficially helpful but also somewhat arrogant in her position of knowledge keeper" (Tancheva 2005, 540). While the reference interview itself could be thought of as a Jedi mind trick (the question you are asking will not give you the answer you are looking for), librarians are not often held in the same esteem in popular culture as Jedi Knights are in the Star Wars universe.

These images of an arrogant, unapproachable keeper of books or the smart/sexy/shushing librarian can often serve as a barrier to patron-librarian interaction. Thus, as with all barriers to providing patrons with the answers to their questions, librarians seek to break them down by using the tools of popular culture to dispel these myths.

The blog *This Is What a Librarian Looks Like* (http://lookslikelibrary science.com) states its purpose as "challenging the stereotype one post at a time." Librarians are invited to submit pictures of themselves in order to illustrate the (diversity) of the profession. Images on the site include librarians skydiving, motorcycling, playing musical instruments, rollerblading, and working in the stacks. There are glamour shots, candid shots, costumed shots, vacation shots, and work shots of male and female librarians, both young and old. Those librarians who wish to focus more on their wardrobe that is "not always buns and sensible shoes" can submit a picture to *Librarian Wardrobe* (www .librarianwardrobe.com), which, according to its description, shows that "librarians at various types of libraries have different styles (and dress codes)."

Marilyn Johnson's 2010 book, *This Book Is Overdue!*, attempts to provide the public with profiles of librarians who do not fit the stereotype, describing tattooed librarians, librarians on the streets providing "radical reference," and librarians embedded in online games and other available media. There is no question that librarians are working to dispel the myth of buns and sensible shoes. The question is whether the public is actually aware. How successfully are librarians immersing themselves in popular culture with these alternate images? Are nonlibrarians becoming more aware of the various types of librarians who are available to help them with their information needs? What can librarians do to expose the general public to the alternate images of a librarian? Some of these questions are addressed in the chapters that follow. Obviously, books and articles and a presence on social media are helpful to the cause. However, another, more personal way for a nonlibrarian to learn that not all librarians fit the same mold is for him or her to have a positive interaction with a librarian either at the reference desk, over the phone, via instant message, or through video chat or social media.

Technology: The Mother of Reinvention

Reinventing Reference aims to define and describe how these interactions are changing and what librarians are doing to embrace the paradigm shift. As we move to a more web-based, online environment for finding information, the image of the librarian as keeper of the books should be dissolving. However, one concern is that the archaic image is not being replaced by one of a savvy online searcher but instead with the picture of a colorful six-letter word that begins with *G* and ends in *e*. Having gained popularity as a search engine, relatively recently with an international presence established in 2000, Google is sometimes seen as competition to library services. An article written in 2005 points out that at the time of publication, "For libraries, Google does have very profound implications, and is accelerating trends that would have developed eventually anyway, such as the digitization of library collections, and a shift to disintermediation which leaves many librarians feeling like fifth wheels, even while it empowers users and seemingly frees them from dependence on library buildings and collections" (Miller, 2005, 2). Google, along with the rest of the Internet, empowers not only users but also information specialists, who can redefine the antique image as keeper of books to finder of information. For example, social media services strengthen communication, conversation, and collaboration while also providing patrons and librarians with entire new frontiers for finding information. The reference librarian of the future should embrace the technology that is being developed in order to strengthen existing skills, skills that many patrons do not even realize are necessary for finding good, authoritative, and accurate information on the World Wide Web.

The purpose of this book is to propose questions and suggest strategies for information professionals regarding the future of reference. *Reinventing Reference* is intended to be inclusive of all aspects of librarianship: public, academic, school, and special collections. While professionals in each of these categories have unique considerations and unique sets of resources according to the primary communities that they serve, they all share a commitment to providing information and services to those communities, and reference is a fundamental—one could argue *the* fundamental—service that all libraries offer. To place *Reinventing Reference* into proper focus, a definition of terms seems in order. What is it that the collaborators of this book are talking about when speaking of "reference" and what "future" is being prognosticated?

The definition of the "reference transaction" as developed by the Reference and User Services Association (RUSA) of the American Library Association states:

> **Reference Transactions** are information consultations in which library staff recommend, interpret, evaluate, and/or use information resources to help others to meet particular information needs. Reference transactions do not include formal instruction or exchanges that provide assistance with locations, schedules, equipment, supplies, or policy statements.
>
> **Reference Work** includes reference transactions and other activities that involve the creation, management, and assessment of information or research resources, tools, and services. (RUSA 2008; emphasis in the original)

RUSA cites other professional organizations' definitions of the terms, including those by the Association of Research Libraries (ARL) and the National Center for Education Statistics (NCES), that are precise and carefully crafted and are important for quantifying substantive, reference exchanges versus simple, informational exchanges (such as library hours and directions). The main ingredient that characterizes a reference exchange is that the information professional is called upon to use his or her expertise and knowledge base in response to the user's query. *Reinventing Reference* draws upon these definitions but also uses the terms in their broadest sense; that is, a reference transaction involves the act of negotiating the information needs of a patron/user with the resources available to meet those needs by an information professional. It also encompasses instruction, as the information professional both guides the patron to and facilitates the use of a resource or guides the patron through the next step of the process to get to a resource. Thus, while the "reference exchange" is exact and quantifiable, the practice of providing reference is an art and its boundaries are porous.

This book is also about the future—the near future, which is just at the doorstep of the present. The act of writing about "the future" is well-known to be a risky business. A trope in contemporary popular culture is the refrain of "Dude, where's … my jetpack?" (Arar 2012). Author John Green writes, "Imagining the future is a kind of nostalgia. … [Y]ou just use the future to escape the present" (Green 2005, 54). "Future-casting" seems to be a lens through which the fears and dreams of a very real "now" are projected. Fears of a total-itarian society, precipitated by the nearly successful rise of Fascism in Europe in the 1930s and 1940s, and the then-current rise of Communism, underlie the near-future dystopia of George Orwell's *1984* (published in 1949). The rapid rise of industrialization at the expense of workers' rights is at the heart of Fritz Lang's dystopian future portrayed in *Metropolis* (released in 1927), wherein oppressed workers of 2026 live and toil underground to serve giant, maw-like machines. A more lighthearted view of the future is evidenced in the Hanna-Barbera cartoon series *The Jetsons* (originally broadcast 1962–1963), which portrays a future in which the booming post–World War II prosperity of the 1950s and 1960s continues on, with even better and more souped-up con-sumer goods and flying cars. Thus, "the future" is a Rorschach test that reveals current concerns. For librarians and library administrators, those current con-cerns center on dire economic realities and the perception of a diminishing role for libraries in the age of Google and Siri, the disembodied "reference librari-an" featured in Apple's iPhones and iPads. These concerns are echoed in this work. However, there is also optimism and the advocacy of the idea that the profession of librarianship and libraries themselves are being reinvented and reshaped as society advances into an exciting new age of information services.

This work, like the ghosts in Dickens's *A Christmas Carol*, harkens to the past, the present, and library reference yet to come. The chapters in Part I, "Un-derstanding Reference," define reference and situate the concept in both his-torical and contemporary contexts. In chapter 1, "A History of Reference," Julie M. Still covers what the chapter title implies, outlining the history of libraries from ancient Alexandria to Andrew Carnegie to Apple. Chapter 2, "Terrorism, Privacy, and Porn: Reference Ethics in the Twenty-First Century," provides the reader with an overview of the professional standards and ethics that have evolved with regard to reference and instruction. Zara Wilkinson and Vibiana Bowman Cvetkovic examine the American Library Association as the "major player" in the development of ethical standards and guidelines for the profes-sion. In chapter 3, "The Real Reference Revolution: The Digital Library User," Susan J. Beck examines recent history, specifically how the personal computer and the World Wide Web radically altered the way information is generated and consumed. Beck also explores how libraries and librarians are interpreted and presented in both pop culture and popular media and looks at how these public perceptions influence the funding and policies that affect libraries.

Part II, "Reference 2.0," examines the current state of library services. Chapters 4 through 7 present the state of reference for the various kinds of libraries: academic ("Reference Service Trends and Forecasts for Academic Librarianship," by Gary Golden); school ("The State of Reference in School Libraries," by Lawrence V. Ghezzi and Walter Johnson); public ("The Future of Public Library Reference," by Justin Hoenke); and special collections ("The Central Image: The Future of Reference in Academic Arts Libraries," by Sara Harrington), respectively. Each chapter details current issues, delineates problems, and offers solutions.

Part III, "'Dude, Where's My Jetpack?' Near Future of Reference," is a look at the future of library services. Chapter 8, "Whither Libraries? User-Driven Changes in the Future of Reference," by John Gibson, is an examination of emerging technologies and new methods of delivery for information services that are being driven by user demand. In chapter 9, "Future World: Strategic Challenges for Reference in the Coming Decade," Stephen Abram explores new paradigms of reference and poses questions regarding the delivery and implementation of those services to librarians and library administrators. Finally, in "Coda" by John Gibson, the author prognosticates as to how reference may be delivered in 2052.

This book went to press in 2014. As librarians know, and as they tell beginning researchers as they guide them through the research process, in this digital age, as soon as something appears in print, it is already out of date. It is our hope that continued dialogue on the topic will forge new solutions.

Finally, this book is not just for librarians and library administrators but for all those concerned about the future of "the library"—indeed, this should be everyone concerned with the future of the next generation of citizens. According to Thomas Jefferson, "Whenever the people are well informed, they can be trusted with their own government; whenever things get so far wrong as to attract their notice, they may be relied on to set them to rights" (Padover 1939, 6). In this information age, the ability to be well-informed means not only access to information but also the ability to find, interpret, and evaluate that information. In short, it means the ability to ask and answer questions in a meaningful way. This is the heart of reference librarianship.

REFERENCES

Arar, Yardena. 2012. "Dude, Where's My Flying Car and Jetpack?" MSNBC.com. Accessed August 11. www.msnbc.msn.com/id/38353006/ns/technology _and_science-tech_and_gadgets/t/dude-wheres-my-flying-car-jetpack/# .UCfJR52PX0M.

Green, John. 2005. *Looking for Alaska*. New York: Dutton.

Harry Potter Wiki. 2012. "Irma Pince." Wikia. Accessed November 24. http://harrypotter.wikia.com/wiki/Irma_Pince.

Johnson, Marilyn. 2010. *This Book Is Overdue! How Librarians and Cybrarians Can Save Us All*. New York: HarperCollins.

Miller, William. 2005. "Introduction: Libraries and Their Interrelationships with Google." In *Libraries and Google*, edited by William Miller and Rita M. Pellen, 1–4. Binghamton, NY: Haworth Information Press.

Padover, Saul K. 1939. *Thomas Jefferson on Democracy*. New York: Appleton-Century.

Peresie, Michelle, and Linda B. Alexander. 2005. "Librarian Stereotypes in Young Adult Literature." *Young Adult Library Services* 4 (1): 24–31.

Raish, Martin. 2011. "Librarians in the Movies: An Annotated Filmography." David O. McKay Library, Brigham Young University. Last updated August 5. http://emp .byui.edu/raishm/films/introduction.html.

RUSA (Reference and User Services Association). 2008. "Definitions of Reference." American Library Association. Approved January 14. www.ala.org/rusa/resources/ guidelines/definitionsreference.

Tancheva, Kornelia. 2005. "Recasting the Debate: The Sign of the Library in Popular Culture." *Libraries and Culture* 40 (4): 530–46.

Part I

UNDERSTANDING REFERENCE

1

A History of Reference

Julie M. Still

Perhaps the best definition of reference librarians was coined by W. W. Bishop in 1915 when he wrote, "they are the interpreters of the library to the public" (134). And yet, he noted that reference librarians were not often considered part of the scholarly content of the library, but instead part of the machinery of the library, like a catalog or a file. Bishop later said of a reference librarian, "he is a lubricant, making the wheels run noiselessly and well. Little glory and less reputation accrue to him" (139).

There are a number of books written on the history of libraries in general, on specific types of libraries, on public and academic libraries, and on how to perform individual library functions, including reference, but there is very little on the history of reference. A bibliography of American library history lists only a page and half of references on the history of public services, and not all of those entries concern reference (Davis and Tucker 1989, 272–73). Several that do are theses. Only two books listed are on the history of reference services, and both are association publications. One of them, Samuel Rothstein's *The Development of Reference Services through Academic Traditions,*

Public Library Practice and Special Librarianship, published by the Association of College and Research Libraries (ACRL) in 1955, is Rothstein's doctoral dissertation. In his book, Rothstein himself comments on the lack of historical and evaluative studies of libraries (1). Standard reference service textbooks offer little or nothing on its history.

Reference service proper, with an official name, may have a set beginning point, but realistically, as long as libraries have existed, there have been people who have been asked the questions "Where is . . . ?" or "How do I find . . . ?" and have done their best to answer. As soon as library collections became so large that patrons could not easily find what they needed, libraries would find someone able to keep track of titles, especially those bound together, on a full-time basis. As collections became larger still, the job became specialized, with librarians keeping track of only part of the library's materials. And yet, while the history of this occupation probably has enough fascinating anecdotes and meaty statistics and stories to fill at least a few books, both scholarly and popular, it remains a subject unmined.

History of Early Libraries

The lives of the greats are chronicled, but the lives of those who stand and wait are often not. All the same, it is provable that librarians came into being not long after libraries. In Babylonian and Assyrian empires a librarian had a title ("Nisu-duppi-satri" or "man of the tablets"), and librarians were named in records as far back as roughly 2,000 BC ("Babylonian and Assyrian Libraries" 1870, 313). While we cannot be certain that the Nisu-duppi-satri was responsible for answering reference questions, it is not unrealistic to imagine that he did answer them. Just as the years BC were turning into AD (or CE), the Portico of Octavia was built and included a library. When the Portico was given to the public, funding was included for library attendants, slaves who had been trained for such work (Thompson 1940, 82–83). When Sulla captured Athens, around 100 BC, he had one of the city's private libraries taken to Rome. Two librarians, Tyrannion (also known as Tyrannio) and Andronicus of Rhodes, were chosen to take care of it (Thompson 1940, 29–30). Tyrannion later arranged Cicero's library (Lerner 1998, 33). The library at Alexandria had such a large staff that the slaves at the lowest rung of library workers were numerous enough to have their own doctor (Thompson 1940, 79). The names of some of the librarians were recorded and are still known, among them Eratosthenes and Aristarchus. Different classifications of library work had different titles, though none translate directly as anything resembling reference librarian (Thompson 1940, 78).

The Middle East, Greece, and Rome were not alone in hosting libraries. China also housed and developed large libraries. In the seventh century, some of the library staff members were women (Lerner 1998, 57). The oldest surviving book on librarianship was written in eleventh-century China by Ch'eng Chu, who outlined the technical aspects of library work but did not include reference among them (Lerner 1998, 58–59). Most of these early libraries had catalogs, by subject in larger libraries and by author or title listing in smaller libraries. The largest, like the library at Alexandria, divided the collection by subject, with librarians and staff dedicated to each area. Royal and monastic libraries had staff assigned to them. Surely those librarians offered a service similar to what current practitioners of this art would call reference, although it was not recorded or discussed as such. Much of their work revolved around copying manuscripts and maintaining existing manuscripts. Jones (1947) provides a list of librarians mentioned in the archives of the monastery at Corbie along with a synopsis of their accomplishments (197). Thus, the works of Gondacer and John the One-Eyed are not lost to history.

Early American society had subscription or private libraries, the forerunner of contemporary public libraries. The larger of these libraries had a designated librarian, though this was not necessarily a full-time job. In some cases, the job involved only unlocking the door for people to enter the room or, in the case of a home-based library, setting aside a room in a house and lighting a fire and providing candles (Stiffler 2011, 390). Although the duties were few, being the librarian and taking care of the library in a home was considered a position of trust and status. When President William Henry Harrison was governor of Illinois, his house served as the location of the local subscription library, and one of his sons was the designated librarian (Peckham 1958, 656). When the Library Company of Philadelphia was formed in 1751, its articles of governance included appointing a clerk, who would serve as librarian, and enumerated the clerk's duties, among which were opening the reading room at set times and lending out books under prescribed circumstances (Lamberton 1918, 197). While these libraries served as cultural centers and social spaces, they were seldom large enough for the librarian to do much more than allow members into the library space and see to the upkeep of the collection.

Development of Reference Desks and Departments

It was not until centuries later, when public libraries began to open to a broader public (the great unwashed, as it were) and academic institutions began to do more rigorous research, that libraries developed what we think of as reference today. Even then, it took some time for that part of librarianship to coalesce as a separate function in the minds of the librarians and library patrons. One of the first separate reference departments was started in Chicago by William Frederick Poole in the late 1800s (Garrison 1979, 29). It is somewhat difficult to understand exactly what that entailed. British libraries in the 1850s were differentiating between the "reference library" and the "lending library" ("Free Public Libraries" 1856, 389). What they meant by those terms related more to the use of the books, ones that could be taken out and ones that were consulted in house, than to the jobs of the people who worked in those parts of the library. By 1881, people were referring to the "reference department" as opposed to the "reading room" at the Chicago Public Library ("Our Chicago Letter" 1881, 196). Library architects were incorporating a reference department into their suggested plans in 1881 ("Construction of Library Buildings" 1881, 138). In general, these reference departments did not refer to the functions of the staff who worked in the departments but to the type of books located there. A history of the Cleveland Public Library published in 1887 states that some books were better suited to staying in the library than to circulating, and those books should be kept in the "Reference Department" (Brett 1887, 58).

However, it is clear that reference work was being done. In 1876, Samuel Swett Green spoke in favor of librarians assisting public library patrons in finding information and establishing a working relationship with them; college librarians adapted his suggestion for creating a teaching role for themselves (Rothstein 1955, 21–22). Green's view that people should be treated with courtesy and assisted in finding the answers to their questions was considered radical (Jackson 1974, 343). In 1882, William Frederick Poole held a meeting with the principals of local Chicago schools to outline a plan wherein the schools would bring students to the public library on a Saturday. The teacher would introduce the students to a particular subject. The librarian would have selected books on that subject from the collection and would tell the students how to further their research ("Letter from Chicago" 1883, 4). Rothstein cites the earliest definition of "reference work" as a speech by William B. Child at the New York Library Club in 1891, but he himself dates the beginning of reference back to 1875 (Rothstein 1955, 3). An 1885 survey of librarians showed that personal service by librarians was more important than finding aids like catalogs and bibliographies (Kaplan 1947, 287). By 1894, the work had become commonplace enough for someone to write a short piece on the life of a reference librarian for *The Critic* ("The Lounger" 1894, 277), which sounds exactly like the sort of comments one hears from reference librarians today. In 1898, the new library at Princeton included a room for the reference librarian ("New Buildings of Princeton" 1898, 283). Yale was somewhat slower; it did not appoint a reference librarian until 1900 (Rothstein 1955, 34). When writing of Andrew Carnegie's gift to the country's libraries, Melvil Dewey himself, the father of the Dewey Decimal System, foresaw the growth of reference librarianship. He said that already, in 1901, it was impossible for any one librarian to know all of a library's collections and that reference librarians would need to specialize in subject areas, forming what he called a "library faculty" (Dewey 1901, 144).

Nor were American librarians alone in this. Special and other types of research libraries in other parts of the world were also expanding their offerings, which required hiring more staff and allowing librarians to specialize in particular subject areas. The reference reading room in the British Museum was opened by Richard Garnett, who became the superintendent of the reading room in 1875. He also had electric lights installed (Koch 1914, 259). As in American libraries, the title "reference librarian" was not used, but reference was certainly being done. When Garnett stepped down from supervising the reading room in 1884, he remarked upon some of the odd queries that had come his way, such as requests to see the signature of Jesus ("In the British Museum" 1885). Sir John McAlister, who became the resident librarian at the Royal Medical and Chirurgical Society (later the Royal Society of Medicine) in London in 1885, decided that the library would provide literature searches for those who could not come to the library in person ("Library of the Royal" 1953).

By 1915, most research libraries offered reference service with some staff devoted solely to that work (Rothstein 1955, 40). Special libraries were also developing reference collections. New York was the first state to institute a legislative reference department, in 1890, and other states followed suit (Fisher 1909, 223). In 1910, the national Civic Federation's Conference on Uniform State Legislation passed a resolution encouraging all states to open legislative reference bureaus (Cleland 1910). Indeed, the level of involvement in legislative matters grew to such an extent that one of the best-known state legislative directors, Charles McCarthy of Wisconsin, was accused of having "undue influence" over lawmaking in that state (Rothstein 1990, 408). Academic libraries (and likely larger public libraries) further specialized as time went on. Reference librarians became less focused on making library materials accessible, a task more suited to catalogers, and more focused on acting as intermediaries between professors, students, and the materials they needed to complete assignments (Fenton 1938, 154). Wagers (1978) offers a well-researched but brief overview of the shifts in the approach to and view of reference work in the twentieth century. As early as 1911, expectations for reference librarians, especially in academic libraries, were high, as this quote from the annual report of the College and Reference Committee (1911) of the American Library Association (ALA) demonstrates: "The reference librarian must needs possess a larger grasp of information than any professor, for this member of the staff must know in general all that the faculty knows in detail" (259). This attitude is also reflected in an article by E. C. Richardson of Princeton University that he presented to the ALA in 1916, wherein he wrote, "There is no single unit in a university education more valuable than being shown by a reference librarian how to find the best book on a given topic or class of topics" (9).

History of Reference in Library Education

In the 1880s, larger libraries with reference assistants began to offer formal training in patron assistance. Public libraries in Boston, Chicago, St. Louis, and Milwaukee, along with Harvard and the Boston Athenaeum, were among the early adopters (Kaplan 1947, 287). The School Libraries Section of the ALA convened a Committee on Standardizing Library Courses in Normal Schools, which published a report in 1915. The list included a class called "The Reference Course, or, the Use of the Library and Books" ("School Library Section" 1915, 280). By 1916, ten states required special training for school librarians, and reference work was frequently mentioned as a necessary skill (Walter et al. 1916). The author of an early British text on reference notes in the preface that starting in 1938, students in accredited library programs will be required to pass a test in "library stock and assistance to readers" (McColvin and McColvin 1936, v).

In the textbooks used in contemporary reference classes, there is very little on the history of reference. A 1944 text published by the ALA, *Introduction to Reference Work* by Margaret Hutchins, devotes a little over one page to a definition of reference work but does not provide any historical material.

William Katz, whose two-volume *Introduction to Reference Work* has become a standard and is currently in its eighth edition, changed the introductory history section. The first edition included a short (six-page) overview of the development of reference service, which notes that Rothstein's 1955 work is the only history of reference available (Katz 1969, 2:5–11). In the eighth edition, the history of printed works and reference librarianship is covered in just slightly more than one page. Another text, *Introduction to Library Public Services* by Evans, Amodeo, and Carter, has also gone through several editions. In the sixth edition, published in 1999, there is a short, four-page introduction and history of reference.

Reference in Professional Library Associations

Formal reference service and the ALA began around the same time. Samuel Swett Green, referenced previously as an earlier proponent of reference service, expounded on his theories in the first volume of the newly formed association's official publication, then the *Library Journal*, in 1876 (Kaplan 1947, 286). The Public Library Association (PLA) published professional standards in 1933; these were the first such published guidelines. The two-page statement noted that reference was a valuable part of library service (Phelps 1957, 282). The 1943 revision was more than ninety pages long (Martin 1972, 164). However, the Reference and Adult Services Division (now Reference and User Services Association) was not formed until 1957, when the reference sections of the PLA and the ACRL combined (Hansen 1995). The PLA, formed in 1944, grew out of the Public Library Section, which had a Reference Committee going back at least as far as 1929. It is in the academic area that reference librarians found their first home with the ALA. The College Library Section was started in 1890 and renamed the College and Reference Section in 1897 (Davis 2003).

Conclusion

Reference librarians appear to show little interest in the history of their profession. This may seem odd in a profession whose work is centered on curiosity. It may be, however, that while the tools used have changed, clay tablets to hand-copied books to mass-produced printing to computer databases to the

Internet, the nature of the work has not. Reference librarians and their fore-bears have always done their best to connect the inquirer to the best source available. Since reference work has been written about as such, the themes running through those commentaries are identical to the ones written about in library blogs and peer-reviewed articles today. Those include the surprising inability of people to locate materials in the library, the reluctance to ask questions, a lack of respect from other professions and from the general public, and the constant lack of funds. Given that there is, as the saying goes, nothing new under the sun, reference librarians could prefer not to look backward, at a profession unchanged except for some of the tools used, and instead prefer to dwell within the moment, answering questions as they arrive. The presence of professional organizations and organized, standardized education provides structure and a means of interacting with like-minded individuals. What is clear is that the history of reference remains a field available for study and in need of more in-depth research.

REFERENCES

"Babylonian and Assyrian Libraries." 1870. *North British Review* 51 (January): 305–24.

Bishop, W. W. 1915. "The Theory of Reference Work." *Bulletin of the American Library Association* 9 (4): 134–9.

Brett, W. H. 1887. "Rise and Growth of the Cleveland Public Library."*Magazine of Western History* 7 (1): 55–61.

Cleland, Ethel. 1910. "Legislative Reference." *American Political Science Review* 4 (2): 218–20.

[College and Reference Committee.] 1911. *Bulletin of the American Library Association* 5 (4): 251–63.

"Construction of Library Buildings." 1881. *American Architect and Building News* 10 (299): 131–8.

Davis, Donald G., Jr., and John Mark Tucker. 1989. *American Library History: A Comprehensive Guide to the Literature.* Santa Barbara, CA: ABC-CLIO.

Davis, Mary Ellen. 2003. "ARCL History." In *Encyclopedia of Library and Information Science*, 2nd ed., 163–73. New York: Marcel Dekker.

Dewey, Melvil. 1901. "The Future of the Library Movement in the United States in the Light of Andrew Carnegie's Recent Gift." *Journal of Social Science* November 1: 139–57.

Evans, G. Edward, Anthony J. Amodeo, and Thomas L. Carter. 1999. *Introduction to Library Public Services.* 6th ed. Englewood, CO: Libraries Unlimited.

Fenton, Dorothy Maie. 1938. "The Reference Librarian." *Journal of Higher Education* 9 (3): 153–6.

Fisher, Edgar A. 1909. "Legislative Reference." *American Political Science Review* 3 (2): 223–6.

"Free Public Libraries in Great Britain." 1856. *American Publishers' Circular and Literary Gazette* 2 (27): 389.

Garrison, Dee. 1979. *Apostles of Culture: The Public Librarian and American Society, 1876–1920.* New York: Free Press.

Hansen, Andrew. 1995. "RASD: Serving Those Who Serve the Public." *RQ* 34 (3): 314–38.

Hutchins, Margaret. 1944. *Introduction to Reference Work.* Chicago: American Library Association.

"In the British Museum." 1885. *New York Times,* February 7.

Jackson, Sidney L. 1974. *Libraries and Librarianship in the West.* New York: McGraw-Hill.

Jones, Leslie Weber. 1947. "The Scriptorium at Corbie I: The Library." *Speculum* 22 (2): 191–204.

Kaplan, Louis. 1947. "The Early History of Reference Service in the United States." *Library Review* 11 (3): 286–90.

Katz, William A. 1969. *Introduction to Reference Work.* 2 vols. New York: McGraw-Hill.

Koch, Theodore W. 1914. "Some Old-Time Old-World Librarians." *North American Review* 200 (705): 244–59.

Lamberton, E. V. 1918. "Colonial Libraries of Philadelphia." *Pennsylvania Magazine of History and Biography* 42 (3): 193–234.

Lerner, Fred. 1998. *Libraries through the Ages.* New York: Continuum.

"Letter from Chicago." 1883. *New York Evangelist* 54 (31): 4–5.

"Library of the Royal Society of Medicine." 1953. *British Medical Journal* 2 (4848): 1262–6.

"The Lounger." 1894. *The Critic: A Weekly Review of Literature and the Arts* 21 (635): 276–7.

Martin, Lowell A. 1972. "Standards for Public Libraries." *Library Trends* 21 (2): 164–177.

McColvin, Lionel R., and Eric R. McColvin. 1936. *Library Stock and Assistance to Readers: A Textbook.* London: Grafton.

"The New Buildings of Princeton University." 1898. *Scientific American* 79 (18): 282–4.

"Our Chicago Letter." 1881. *Western Christian Advocate* 48 (25): 196.

Peckham, Howard H. 1958. "Books and Reading on the Ohio Valley Frontier." *Mississippi Valley Historical Review* 44 (4): 649–63.

Phelps, Rose B. 1957. "Reference Services in Public Libraries." *Wilson Library Bulletin* 32 (4): 281–5.

Richardson, E. C. 1916. "The Place of the Library in a University." *Bulletin of the American Library Association* 10 (1): 1–13.

Rothstein, Samuel. 1955. *The Development of Reference Services through Academic Traditions, Public Library Practice and Special Librarianship.* Chicago: Association of College and Research Libraries.

———. 1990. "The Origins of Legislative Reference Services in the United States." *Legislative Studies Quarterly* 15 (3): 401–11.

"School Library Section." 1915. *Bulletin of the American Library Association* 9 (4): 276–87.

Stiffler, Stuart A. 2011. "Books and Reading in the Connecticut Western Reserve: The Small-Settlement Social Library, 1800–1860." *Libraries and the Cultural Record* 46 (4): 388–411.

Thompson, James Westfall. 1940. *Ancient Libraries.* Hamden, CT: Archon Books.

Wagers, Robert. 1978. "American Reference Theory and the Information Dogma." *The Journal of Library History* 13 (3): 265–81.

Walter, Frank, K., Harriet A. Wood, Mary C. Richardson, W. D. Johnston, Effie M. Power, Ida M. Mendenhall, and Mary E. Hall. 1916. "Report of the Committee on Training Courses for School Librarians." *Bulletin of the American Library Association* 10 (4): 219–27.

2

Terrorism, Privacy, and Porn
Reference Ethics in the Twenty-First Century

Zara Wilkinson and Vibiana Bowman Cvetkovic

n the seminal work *Our Enduring Values*, Michael Gorman (2000) outlined eight "central values" of librarianship: stewardship, service, intellectual freedom, rationalism (organizing principles for materials, procedures, and programs), literacy and learning, equity of access to recorded knowledge and information, privacy, and democracy (26–27). His formulation, which expressed his own vision of librarianship, was founded on the values and ethics scholarship of eminent librarians S. R. Ranganathan, Jesse Shera, Samuel Rothstein, and Lee Finks (18). In his discussion of Finks's *Taxonomy of Values*, Gorman wrote that positive values of librarianship such as idealism and optimism are threatened by rival values such as "bureaucracy, anti-intellectualism, and nihilism" (26). Gorman also detailed the toll that these negative values take on the profession. He noted that bureaucratic mind-sets are endemic because of the nature of the profession, which embraces a "desire for order and regular procedure." The other two rival values are arguably more worrisome:

> There is an anti-intellectual tone to much of the discourse about tech-
> nology that can be found in statements that equate the Internet and
> a research library or Web surfing and serious reading. . . . Nihilism is
> the philosophy of the despairing, and a librarian who loses faith in the
> future of libraries or the value of librarianship is succumbing to that
> despair. (26)

The negative influences of bureaucracies, anti-intellectualism, and nihilism
described by Gorman resonate with new meaning more than ten years after
his book first appeared. Will they continue to resonate into the near future?

This chapter examines the professional ethics and values that shape reference librarianship in the twenty-first century. The authors will attempt to
answer three questions: What are the extant frameworks that inform ethical
reference librarianship? What are some of the most important ethical issues
facing librarians today? Finally, are the current guidelines flexible enough to
accommodate the future of reference work in a post-9/11, increasingly technological, and perhaps postliterate culture? The discussion begins with a look at
current ethical standards regarding reference librarianship and an examination of how they reflect the values of the profession.

The Frameworks

Many professional library associations in the United States make public their
code of ethics or a list of ethical principles. The Special Libraries Association
(SLA), the Medical Library Association (MLA), and the American Association of Law Libraries (AALL), for example, each has a code of ethics that is
tailored to the unique responsibilities of its organizational members. The "gold
standard" for ethical codes in librarianship, however, is the "Code of Ethics of
the American Library Association" (ALA 2008; hereinafter Code). The ALA
is the main organizing force within the profession; as an entity it encompasses
all aspects of librarianship. For that reason, the ALA's Code will be the primary document discussed in this section.

At the outset it should be noted that the premier organization devoted
specifically to reference librarianship is the Reference and User Services Association (RUSA), a division of the American Library Association. RUSA, as
a professional body, has developed a series of guidelines to inform the practice
of librarians who provide reference and research services to users in all types

of libraries. These guidelines address topics as varied as the behavioral performance of reference service providers, the implementation of virtual reference services, and responses to questions in the fields of medicine, law, and business. The RUSA (2000) "Guidelines for Information Services" outlines a series of service goals for reference and information service providers. These service goals are divided into the following topics: services, resources, access, personnel, evaluation, and ethics. In regard to ethics, however, RUSA defers to the ALA and asserts that the Code "governs the conduct of all staff members providing information service."

The Code lays out the core values of the organization and "embodies the ethical responsibilities of the profession in this changing information environment." Revised in 2008, it is made up of eight broad principles:

I. We provide the highest level of service to all library users through appropriate and usefully organized resources; equitable service policies; equitable access; and accurate, unbiased, and courteous responses to all requests.

II. We uphold the principles of intellectual freedom and resist all efforts to censor library resources.

III. We protect each library user's right to privacy and confidentiality with respect to information sought or received and resources consulted, borrowed, acquired, or transmitted.

IV. We respect intellectual property rights and advocate balance between the interests of information users and rights holders.

V. We treat co-workers and other colleagues with respect, fairness, and good faith, and advocate conditions of employment that safeguard the rights and welfare of all employees of our institutions.

VI. We do not advance private interests at the expense of library users, colleagues, or our employing institutions.

VII. We distinguish between our personal convictions and professional duties and do not allow our personal beliefs to interfere with fair representation of the aims of our institutions or the provision of access to their information resources.

VIII. We strive for excellence in the profession by maintaining and enhancing our own knowledge and skills, by encouraging the professional development of co-workers, and by fostering the aspirations of potential members of the profession.

The first four principles address issues of access and the rights of individuals. These include providing the highest level of service and equitable access, upholding the principles of intellectual freedom, guaranteeing users' rights to privacy, and balancing the needs of users of information with those of intellectual property rights holders. The second group of four principles addresses ethical workplace behavior for librarians. These include advocating for safe and respectful employment conditions, not advancing private interests at the expense of library users, maintaining a balance between personal convictions and professional duties, and always striving for excellence in the profession of librarianship.

The Code successfully lays out the basic tenets of ethical librarianship in the United States. However, applying the Code to practice can be complicated since it is intended to provide guidance to information professionals by articulating a shared set of beliefs rather than to dictate behavior. Problems can arise when specific situations require librarians to navigate conflicting convictions, loyalties, and values. As stated in the Code documentation, "Ethical dilemmas occur when values are in conflict." For example, a librarian who is asked to help a patron download copyrighted media will find himself or herself in an ethical dilemma; providing the patron with an "accurate, unbiased, and courteous" answer may conflict with attempts to protect intellectual property rights. In another instance, a patron who uses the library's "equitable access" and anti-censorship policies to view pornographic material on library computers may subject library employees to materials they find offensive, thus creating a hostile work environment. The patron's use of library terminals would therefore conflict with ALA's stated intent to "advocate conditions of employment that safeguard the rights and welfare of all employees of our institutions."

The Code may also conflict with a librarian's personal beliefs or with federal, state, or local laws. As in the earlier example, a librarian who does not wish to facilitate copyright infringement might be uncomfortable allowing computer access to a patron who has expressed the intention to illegally download copyrighted material. Similarly, a librarian who intends to "protect each library user's right to privacy and confidentiality" would struggle with a law enforcement officer's request for personal information about a patron. In "Ethics and the Reference Librarian," Charles Bunge (1999) singles out ethical norms based on personal religious and political beliefs as the most likely to influence librarians' professional practices:

Purely personal ethical norms, such as those based on religious or political beliefs . . . cannot restrict professional obligations in the librarian's practice. Conflicts between obligations to the reference client and
personal religious beliefs (e.g., aversion to certain religious practices
or birth control methods) must be resolved in favor of the obligation to
assist the client diligently and with independence of judgment. (37–38)

Here Bunge evokes the Code's seventh principle, which decrees that librarians
must "distinguish between our personal convictions and professional duties
and [can] not allow our personal beliefs to interfere with fair representation of
the aims of our institutions or the provision of access to their information resources." When providing reference and information services, librarians strive
to be impartial and professional, leaving their opinions and values in the realm
of the personal.

The interlocking themes of neutrality, equality, and freedom from censorship are threaded throughout the Code. Contemporary librarians must balance these professional obligations with their personal, political, religious, and
ethical beliefs in a landscape that has become progressively more diverse and
complex. The next section explores that landscape and some of the professional challenges that librarians may face.

Reference Librarianship in the New Millennium:
New Problems and New Challenges

In an increasingly technological world, librarians struggle to define the ethics
of service and access. This section considers some of the most important issues
faced by contemporary reference librarians as they work to serve their publics
and constituencies. The issues to be examined are grouped into the following
broad categories: access, privacy, and intellectual freedom.

Access

For a variety of reasons—budgets and changing technologies, to name a cou-
ple—the online delivery of library services has become both prevalent and
important. Databases and catalogs are online, and reference is delivered via

"new" platforms and formats, including chat, e-mail, video chat, and social media. The increased usage of online information services raises a number of issues, and one of the most important is the question of accessibility. The Code specifically states that librarians will provide "equitable access" for all requests for information. A key question for virtual library services is how to make the research experience equitable for every user with regard to instruction, reference exchanges, and access to scholarly literature (monographs, reference materials, and journals). In this discussion, the term "accessibility" will be used in the broadest sense of the word. Barriers to resources are encountered not only by those patrons with physical or mental disabilities but also by patrons subject to socioeconomic factors such as limited access to technology or limited computer or language skills. Access—the ability to engage fully in civic life without barriers—is a civil right protected by the Americans with Disabilities Act of 1990. Indeed, as is particularly pertinent to this discussion, access to educational opportunities is protected by this act and by Section 504 of the Rehabilitation Act of 1973.

In higher education, the question of equitable access has become a high-profile issue. Since the turn of the twenty-first century, the makeup of a "typical" undergraduate class has changed dramatically. Veterans from Iraq and Afghanistan are returning and enrolling in online and traditional programs; this group includes wounded vets, many in need of special accommodations (Freking 2013). Precise statistics on veterans with disabilities currently enrolled in post–secondary education classes are difficult to come by due to privacy concerns and regulations; however, a 2008 Rand report indicated that the number may be as high as 25 percent (Madaus, Miller, and Vance 2009, 14). A 2012 *Time* cover story on online higher education presented a profile of the new undergraduate and included several interesting statistics. Today's college student is more in need of remedial classes (36 percent in 2007 as compared to 28 percent in 2000), less economically advantaged, and older. In 2010–2011, 8.9 million students came from low-income housing, as opposed to 176,000 in 1973–1974. Twenty-nine percent were nineteen or older in 2011, as opposed to 14 percent in 1967 (Ripley 2012, 32–41). The changing demographics of the undergraduate experience are further reflected in the fact that racial/ethnic minorities and nonresident aliens now account for 36 percent of all undergraduates. While this figure is still low compared to overall population demographics, it is steadily increasing (McPherson 2010, 33–40).

In her survey of online access to library materials and current law, Camilla Fulton (2011) wrote that barriers to library services exist for a significant segment of the American population and that "nearly 24.5 million people in the United States are unable to retrieve information from library websites" due to visual or hearing impairments (38). Fulton noted that while education rights are protected for persons with disabilities, no federal laws cover web accessibility and (as of 2011, when the article was published) only seventeen states had laws that ensured such access (37). Fulton concluded that although universal web access is a costly and time-consuming enterprise, it is one that should have priority with librarians: "As gatekeepers of information and research resources librarians should want to be the first to provide unrestricted and unhindered access to all patrons despite their ability" (38). Providing such access is the ethical thing to do.

Andromeda Yelton (2012) noted that web accessibility is limited by socio-economic factors; "the digital divide is not just about who has a computer and who doesn't. It's about what *kind* of Internet we experience on our different devices" (8). Yelton wrote that, according to the Pew Internet and American Life Project of 2010, 80 percent of all American adults own a cell phone and 40 percent of those have smart phones with Internet capability (5). According to this Pew study:

> There has been a steady increase in wireless Internet access across most demographic groups, with the largest increases among young adults and people with household incomes under $30,000 per year. . . . 12 percent of adults go online wirelessly using cell phones only! (7)

Based on the data from the study, Yelton concluded that those who have cell-only access to the Internet are "disproportionately likely to be on the disadvantaged side of the digital divide" (7). An unintended consequence of the cell-only Internet experience is that users have more difficulty reading PDFs, navigating complicated webpages, and filling out forms. According to Yelton, this type-of-access–socioeconomic divide has "moral significance" for librarians.

Privacy

The third tenet in the Code concerns the right to privacy and confidentiality for the patron: "We protect each library user's right to privacy and confidentiality with respect to information sought or received and resources consulted, borrowed, acquired, or transmitted." In a post-9/11 American society, the fear of terrorism—both domestic and international—has created challenges to librarians' ability to uphold this tenet. One of the biggest challenges has been the passage of the USA PATRIOT Act.

The Uniting and Strengthening America by Providing Appropriate Tools Required to Intercept and Obstruct Terrorism Act of 2001 (commonly known as the PATRIOT Act) was signed into law forty-five days after the September 11 attacks on New York, Washington, and Flight 93 (which crashed in Shanksville, Pennsylvania). Section 215 of the act gives federal agents the power to obtain National Security Letters issued by a FISA (Foreign Intelligence and Surveillance Act) court that they can then use to access patrons' library records (including computer records). Library employees are prohibited from disclosing to those patrons that their records have been requested. In 2011, Congress passed, and President Obama signed into law, a four-year extension of the act, which included the controversial library provision.

The troubling power of the PATRIOT Act is just the most recent of various government attempts at library surveillance that have surfaced during different crises in modern American history. Other such initiatives include attacks on the privacy of patron records and attempts to censor collections during the anti-Communism fervor of the McCarthy era and the Library Awareness Program, which was conducted by the FBI (Federal Bureau of Investigation) during the 1980s. The "Awareness Program" was a counterintelligence operation conducted in public and academic libraries:

> The goals of the program were to restrict foreigners' access to unclassified scientific information in libraries and to recruit librarians and library staff into reporting on the use of scientific information by foreigners, especially Russian or Eastern Europeans. (Bowman 2003, 6)

For a detailed look at this fascinating piece of library history, see Herbert Foerstel's (1991) book *Surveillance in the Stacks: The FBI's Library Awareness Program*.

Librarians, as individuals and through organizations, have reacted to these ethical challenges in fearless ways. In 1950, during the height of the McCarthy era, librarian Ruth Brown was fired for insubordination when she refused to remove "subversive" materials from the collection of the Bartesville Public Library in Oklahoma. Ms. Brown was supported by both the American Civil Liberties Union (ACLU) and the ALA. Although she was not reinstated (she went on to have a career as a public librarian in Colorado), she was recognized as a hero of intellectual freedom. Brown's story was popularized in the feature film *Storm Center* (1956), which starred Bette Davis. In the late 1990s, the Oklahoma Library Association's Social Responsibility Roundtable founded the Ruth Brown Award to honor her memory (Bowman 2003, 6).

According to the ALA's (2010) *Intellectual Freedom Manual*, the Library Awareness Program was exposed by the *New York Times* in 1987. Public awareness was raised by various librarians in New York who had been contacted by the FBI. They brought the issue to the attention of the New York Library Association and then the ALA: "In response the Intellectual Freedom Committee issued an advisory statement describing the FBI's actions and recommending that libraries oppose any such requests based on ALA policies" (ALA 2010, 271). More recently, librarians concerned with the implications of the PATRIOT Act have been very vocal about their opinions since the act's original passage in 2001. In 2003, Attorney General John Ashcroft mocked librarians as "hysterics" (Lichtbau 2003, 23). The ALA's Office for Intellectual Freedom responded by selling "Another 'Hysteric' Librarian for Freedom" buttons to raise awareness and to support intellectual freedom initiatives (Samek 2007, 53). The ALA continues to be vigilant in educating librarians and the public about the PATRIOT Act and navigating the difficult ethical shoals between the Scylla of lawful government compliance and the Charybdis of defending privacy rights.

While the PATRIOT Act is still a concern, librarians will continue to be challenged by new privacy issues. For example, a future debate might inform the library privacy rights of undocumented immigrants and whether it is legal to provide services to them with state and local tax dollars. Although standards and codes can provide ethical guidelines, and organizations such as the ALA and the ACLU can provide organizational clout, on the front lines of library service, it will be the individual librarian who must take the first stand.

Intellectual Freedom

The Code declares that the organization "uphold[s] the principles of intellectual freedom." Intellectual freedom, in the context of the library environment, refers to the belief that all library users should have "the right to seek and receive information on all subjects from all points of view without restriction and without having the subject of one's interest examined or scrutinized by others" (Morgan 2006, 3). A guarantee of intellectual freedom is therefore a guarantee that any library user should be permitted to access any kind of information without obstruction from personnel or from the collection itself (in the form of censorship or selective acquisition). Experiments conducted by Robert Hauptman and Robert Dowd demonstrate the complexity of upholding the tenets of intellectual freedom and illustrate situations in which many librarians might find themselves experiencing a crisis of ethics.

In 1976, then–graduate student Robert Hauptman published an article titled "Professionalism or Culpability? An Experiment in Ethics." Hauptman's article detailed an experiment in which he visited six public and seven academic libraries where he requested from the librarians information on how to build a small explosive device. He then specified that he was particularly interested in whether a small amount of explosive would blow up a house. Although one academic librarian refused to help because of institutional policies—that is, because he was not a student at the college—none declined his request for information on ethical grounds. In the 1980s, Robert Dowd repeated Hauptman's experiment with slightly different details. Instead of explosives, he inquired about how to freebase cocaine (Dowd 1990). He dressed casually, changed his speech patterns, and purposely acted slightly suspect. As in the Hauptman experiment, none of the librarians he approached refused to help him, although some were perhaps less helpful than they could have been. For Dowd, librarians consulted vertical files, periodical indexes, and books in search of an answer. One accompanied him to the stacks and searched book indexes on his behalf. Many "seemed truly sorry" when they could not find what he needed (488).

The experiments of Hauptman and Dowd produced nearly identical results, but the researchers came to very different conclusions. Hauptman was critical of the librarians' ethical decision making, stating that they had given "the question, within an ethical context, little thought" and "appeared to abjure responsibility to society in favor of responsibility to their role of librarian" (Hauptman 1976, 627). While Dowd too expected to be disappointed in librarians who complied with his request, he eventually came to a different conclusion: "Freebasing cocaine may not be an accepted practice even in our occasionally liberal society, but anyone in this free country should certainly have the right to read about how it is done" (Dowd 1990, 492). These librarians, he came to believe, were correct not to deny aid based on either the appearance of the requesting patron or their own opinions on the appropriateness of the information need. In his article, Dowd supplies some reasons why perfectly law-abiding citizens might have asked a question identical to his own: "A medical student might have elaborated upon a need to know just how cocaine users were abusing their bodies. A writer might have elaborated upon a need for accuracy in a paper he was currently working on" (492). Such a question might also be asked as preparation for an opinion or research paper, a chemistry assignment, the production of a film or play, or out of idle curiosity.

The experiments of Hauptman and Dowd were primarily concerned with whether or not individuals were able to access potentially dangerous or illegal information from libraries. Intellectual freedom issues such as these, while always important, have taken on new significance in recent years. If Robert Hauptman were to ask for assistance finding information about explosive devices today, for example, many librarians might hesitate. The 9/11 attacks dramatically altered the political landscape in the United States and introduced an awareness of terrorism into mainstream American culture. Providing an answer to a reference question regarding explosive devices or the mechanics of other forms of terrorism might understandably conflict with a librarian's personal ethics and cause him or her to experience doubt, distress, or fear. Situations like this must be considered in discussions about what constitutes ethical behavior in contemporary reference librarianship.

Many believe, in the words of Charles Bunge (1999), that it is "unethical to assist a patron to commit an illegal act or one that is immoral according to the values of society" (38). However, asking for information about an illegal act is not in and of itself an illegal act, nor is it necessarily a declaration of intent to commit an illegal act. Moreover, the average librarian is not equipped to determine the legality of a particular instance of behavior, let alone the legality of behavior that may or may not occur in the future. As Dowd (1990) asks, "Where is the omniscient librarian who can foresee what people will do with the information that may be found in libraries?" (491).

Conclusions and Considerations for the Near Future

Twenty-first-century librarians are constantly navigating complex situations, weighing the ethical standards of the profession against their personal beliefs. The ALA's Code is clear. Libraries must ensure equitable service policies and access. Librarians should be expected to provide "accurate, unbiased, and courteous responses" to reference questions and requests. They must "resist all efforts to censor library resources." They have a responsibility to protect each patron's rights in matters of privacy and confidentiality, particularly in regard to books checked out and resources consulted. However, as previously discussed, librarians may find themselves in situations in which a commitment to service and ethical behavior may conflict with personal religious and political views, legal concerns, and broader questions of morality.

The authors of this chapter set themselves the task of addressing three questions about ethics and reference librarianship. Thus, guidelines and ethical frameworks were defined; current issues were outlined; and the responses by librarians—both individual and organizational—were analyzed. Based on current knowledge and practice, how might library ethics guide professionals in the near future?

Prognostication is a notoriously tricky business, as evidenced by forecasts of impending events such as the Millennium or Y2K bug (scenarios of mayhem caused by the inability of computers to process the change in calendar numbering to the 2000s) and the more recent worries over the Mayan calendar prophesying the end of the world on December 21, 2012. However, some fairly safe forecasts can be made through a look at statistical trends that have been gleaning headlines in the popular press. Over the next twenty years, America will become "grayer." The first of the baby boomers began turning sixty-five in 2011. As this large cohort becomes seniors, there will be more demands on library services to accommodate their special needs. America is also becoming more diverse:

> More than one third of its population belongs to a minority group, and
> Hispanics are the fastest-growing segment. . . . Even more telling for
> the future: 44% of children under age 18 and 47% of children under the
> age of five are now from minority families. (Christie 2009)

Demands for dual-language materials and collection development that is culturally sensitive to the needs of multicultural clientele will continue to be a priority. The demand for e-books will continue to expand in both public and academic libraries, and collection building will need to keep pace with this demand. A recent survey in *Library Journal* noted that in a one-year period—from 2010 to 2011—the average number of e-books in public libraries increased 184 percent and in academic libraries, 93 percent (Miller 2011, 32). This "dramatic shift" marks a trend to the digital that will continue. Finally, there is a prevalent notion among scholars of popular culture that society is moving into a postliterate era:

In the last 20 years the notion that images overpower words, and the belief that a decreasing lexical literacy among the young has been off-set by a increasing visual literacy, has been repeated often enough to become accepted wisdom. (Griffin 2008, 113)

As with the other trends noted previously, this shift to an increased demand for multimedia will necessitate changes in equipment and in collections. In addition, a new emphasis on the importance of critical-thinking skills with re-gard to media literacy and visual literacy will have an impact on both reference and bibliographic instruction.

Will extant codes provide sufficient guidance as society moves into an uncertain future? Yes, because the Code, like the U.S. Constitution, is straightforward in its values yet broad enough for interpretation. The values encompassed by the Code are reflective of librarianship itself: respect for indi-viduality and freedom of thought. By contrast, a detailed, prescriptive code of behavior would be antithetical to the spirit of the profession because librarian-ship is both an art and a science. Aspects of librarianship, particularly assess-ment and infometrics, lend themselves to quantification and scientific tools. However, other aspects of librarianship are rooted in human interactions, such as the reference interview, and are based on the art of communication. As librarianship continues into a new era, tools may change and "hot button" issues will change. However, the authors feel confident in predicting that the core values of librarianship—respect for the patron and a commitment to safe-guarding intellectual freedom—will remain constant.

REFERENCES

ALA (American Library Association). 2008. "Code of Ethics of the American Library Association." Last amended January 22, 2008. www.ala.org/advocacy/proethics/codeofethics/codeethics.

———. 2010. *Intellectual Freedom Manual*. Chicago: Office of Intellectual Freedom, American Library Association.

Bowman, Vibiana. 2003. "Teaching and Learning in Libraries under the PATRIOT Act: A Very Short History of Library Surveillance." *LIRT News* 26 (2): 1–12.

Bunge, Charles. 1999. "Ethics and the Reference Librarian." *The Reference Librarian* 31 (66): 25–43.

Christie, Les. 2009. "Census: U.S. Becoming More Diverse." CNN Money. Last updated May 14. http://money.cnn.com/2009/05/14/real_estate/rising_minorities/index.htm.

Dowd, Robert. 1990. "I Want to Find Out How to Freebase Cocaine or Yet Another Unobtrusive Test of Reference Performance." *The Reference Librarian* 11 (25–26): 483–93.

Foerstel, Herbert. 1991. *Surveillance in the Stacks: The FBI's Library Awareness Program.* New York: Greenwood Press.

Freking, Kevin. 2013. "Veterans Are Flocking to Enroll in College as Wars Wind Down." *The Huffington Post,* October 17. www.huffingtonpost.com/2013/10/17/veterans -enroll-in-college_n_4117250.html.

Fulton, Camilla. 2011. "Web Accessibility, Libraries, and the Law." *Information Technology and Libraries* 30 (1): 34–43.

Gorman, Michael. 2000. *Our Enduring Values.* Chicago: American Library Association.

Griffin, Michael. 2008. "Visual Competence and Media Literacy: Can One Exist Without the Other?" *Visual Studies* 23 (2): 113–29.

Hauptman, Robert. 1976. "Professionalism or Culpability? An Experiment in Ethics." *Wilson Library Bulletin* 50 (April): 626–7.

Lichtbau, Eric. 2003. "Ashcroft Mocks Librarians and Others Who Oppose Parts of Counterterrorism Law." *The New York Times,* September 16, 23.

Madaus, Joseph, Wayne K. Miller, and Mary Lee Vance. 2009. "Veterans with Disabilities in Postsecondary Education." *Journal of Postsecondary Education and Disability* 22 (1): 10–17.

McPherson, Michael. 2010. "Access and Equity." *The Chronicle of Higher Education,* August 27, 34–40.

Miller, Rebecca. 2011. "Dramatic Growth." *Library Journal* 136 (17): 32–34.

Morgan, Candace. 2006. "Intellectual Freedom: An Enduring and All-Embracing Concept." In *Intellectual Freedom Manual,* 7th ed., compiled by the American Library Association, 3–13. Chicago: Office of Intellectual Freedom, American Library Association.

Ripley, Amanda. 2012. "College Is Dead: Long Live College." *Time* 180 (18): 32–41.

RUSA (Reference and User Services Association). "Guidelines for Information Services." American Library Association. Approved July 2000. www.ala.org/rusa/resources/ guidelines/guidelinesinformation.

Samek, Toni. 2007. *Librarianship and Human Rights: A Twenty-First Century Guide.* Oxford, UK: Chandos Publishing.

Yelton, Andromeda. 2012. "Who Are Smartphone Users?" *Library Technology Reports* 48 (1): 5–8.

The Real Reference Revolution

The Digital Library User

Susan J. Beck

he World Wide Web profoundly changed how people seek and find information. The reference department as place at the end of the twentieth century changed from a physical destination for information seekers and a storage facility for large collections of reference materials to a space filled with computers for both librarians and library users to access the web through the Internet to find the information they seek. Technological advances in telecommunications and computing as well as changes in media formats, storage capacity, and the development of specialized bibliographic tools have altered the rhythms and nature of reference work. The means of interacting with library users have also changed, but the fundamental premise of reference services has withstood the test of time. At the very core of reference services is the notion that librarians help users find the information they need. The librarian remains the intermediary between users and the information they seek, although today they are often seeking information located on the web, not physically located in the library. Everything changed, yet nothing changed.

This chapter reviews the major technological changes that have contributed to the changing face of reference services today. It explores changes in the provision of reference services, from the physical library to redefinition of the types of services provided, including digital reference. It also examines the impact of digital formats on reference collections, instruction (reflecting the realities of the new information world), and library user behaviors and expectations.

The Enabling Change: Automation in Libraries

An excellent overview of the history of library automation is presented in an article by Robert M. Hayes (2009) in the *Encyclopedia of Library and Information Sciences*. Hayes asserted that the need for information in science and technology provided the impetus for the development of automated information management systems. The following time line of innovations in information services is based on time periods defined by Hayes:

1945–1960

- Creation of Science Citation Index allowed scientists to identify citation networks among related papers.

1960–1975

- Development of commercial online services (Dialog, Orbit, and BRS) provided access to reference bibliographic databases.
- Trained librarians acted as the intermediaries for information seekers.
- Online public access catalogs (OPACs) were introduced using machine-readable cataloging (MARC) records.
- OCLC (Online Computer Library Center) and the Research Library Group implemented cooperative interlibrary loan lending.

1975–1990

- Introduction of personal computing occurred with the advent of the PC and Mac.
- OPACs, available in most libraries, allowed access to users worldwide.
- Laser discs, followed by CD-ROMs, introduced the era of end-user searching.
- Widespread use of the Internet and the World Wide Web provided online communication and access to a new world of information.

1990–2008

- Information seekers used search engines to locate information independently.
- Search engines changed from file name indexing (Archie, Gopher, Veronica, and Jughead) to content indexing (WebCrawler, Lycos, and Google).
- Database services moved to the Internet.
- Online reference desks, such as the Internet Public Library, were developed.
- Library-based, subject-specific research guides were developed.

The major innovations in library automation relate to bibliographic control and the desire to simplify access to information. Robert Maxwell (2009) defined bibliographic control as "the process of creation, exchange, preservation, and use of data about information resources" (497). In more basic terms, someone creates information, subject experts create finding aids, and librarians help users discover the information. According to James Rettig (2006), "Technology impacted the process of searching for bibliographic information more frequently than any other aspect of reference" (108).

Rettig (2006) described the changes in the search process that came during the early stages of information technology:

> The processes of searching for citations and evaluating each citation's relevance were conducted simultaneously by the person who would use the information in the cited sources. The advent of electronic databases changed that. The process of searching belonged exclusively to the librarian; the process of evaluating citations was usually shared by the librarian and the patron. Here in a kernel is the most important trend in reference service over the past 30 years. The respective roles and, in some ways, the responsibilities of the reference librarian and the user of reference service changed. (109)

The role of the librarian and the information seeker changed once again following the introduction of the personal computer (PC). As easy-to-use end-user systems were introduced in the form of laser discs and CD-ROMs, information seekers took back sole responsibility for evaluating the information they discovered. As database services subsequently moved to the web, users continued to be in control of the information they found. Information seekers became more independent with each new technological advance, entering into an Internet era characterized by self-service opportunities in all types of Internet-based enterprises.

Changes in the Provision of Reference Services

Library as Place

The library as place and the available library resources used by reference librarians in the latter part of the twentieth century were vastly different from their counterparts today. In large academic libraries, for example, large reference rooms were once populated with rows of index tables, lined with such familiar old friends from the H. W. Wilson Company as *Readers' Guide to Periodical Literature* and the *Social Sciences and Humanities Index*. Row after row of printed reference books made up the reference department's stacks. Huge card catalogs were often housed in separate bibliographic corridors, surrounded by massive national bibliographies, such as the *National Union Catalog* and the *British National Bibliography*. A grand wooden desk took center stage, with librarians imprisoned behind it.

Today, these reference departments no longer have index tables or card catalogs. There are few print indexes. The physical size of reference collections has shrunk. Some libraries continue to staff a physical reference desk, although the desk has totally disappeared from many libraries. If there is a reference desk, a computer connected to the Internet now takes center stage, and it is rare for the librarian to leave the reference desk to consult a paper-based reference source. If a library user physically enters the library, the reference librarian uses a computer with an Internet connection to help the information seeker locate needed information.

Redefining Reference

As noted at the start of this chapter, at the very core of reference services is the notion that librarians help users find the information they need. According to Linda C. Smith (2009), "To mediate between a library user's information needs and the information resources accessible to that user through the library, libraries offer reference services" (4485).

In 1876, Samuel Swett Green first expressed the fundamental principles of reference services. The core functions of reference services remain today a reflection of those ideals first articulated by Green. Although Green described examples of types of questions asked by public library users, David Tyckoson (2011b) offers a more modern interpretation of Green's vision focusing on four distinct functions of a reference librarian: teach people how to use the library and its resources; answer readers' questions; aid readers in the selection of good books; promote the library within the community (9–10). In the past, the traditional modalities of reference were primarily face-to-face and by phone, with an occasional letter. Librarians helped users find information in card catalogs and printed indexes. When students came into the library with specific information needs, reference librarians would demonstrate how to find books using the library's card catalog and how to find articles using printed indexes.

In 2008, the Reference and User Services Association (RUSA), a division of the American Library Association (ALA), redefined reference. In the press release issued by RUSA, Susan J. Beck, RUSA past-president, explained, "RUSA, the foremost organization of reference and information professionals in the world, has redefined reference to reflect the activities of the twenty-first century reference librarian to serve the needs of a new generation of information seekers" (RUSA 2010). RUSA's current definition follows:

> **Reference Transactions** are information consultations in which library staff recommend, interpret, evaluate, and/or use information resources to help others to meet particular information needs. Reference transactions do not include formal instruction or exchanges that provide assistance with locations, schedules, equipment, supplies, or policy statements.
>
> **Reference Work** includes reference transactions and other activities that involve the creation, management, and assessment of information or research resources, tools, and services.
>
> (The following bullets clarify what is meant by terms within the Reference Work definition.)
> - Creation and management of information resources includes the development and maintenance of research collections, research guides, catalogs, databases, web sites, search engines, etc., that patrons can use independently, in-house or remotely, to satisfy their information needs.
> - Assessment activities include the measurement and evaluation of reference work, resources, and services. (RUSA 2008; emphasis in the original)

Transforming Services

Accessibility

Today libraries offer, and users expect, a variety of services that meet the demanding information needs of our 24/7 anywhere, anytime society. Contemporary reference services offer an amazing number of ways for users to contact librarians. The following examples illustrate some of the ways users now communicate their needs to librarians:

- It is 3:00 a.m.; a genealogist, hundreds of miles away, discovers your library has an old family bible and she e-mails you with questions.
- It is 10:00 a.m.; a user approaches the reference desk in a busy library for help with a term paper on the economic impact of immigration on small communities.
- A student in a library café sees a box on your home page where she can ask a question, so instead of going to the reference desk on the other side of the building, she simply starts chatting with a librarian, latte in hand.
- A distance education student in China is having problems using your online catalog and fills out a web-based form to ask questions.
- A prison inmate sends a letter asking for a copy of a newspaper article you have on microfilm.
- A student sixty miles away calls the library about an item on reserve.
- A businessman connects to the library from his smart phone using a library app.
- A student texts the library to find out the hours it is open, and although the service is down for the evening, the student receives an automatic message indicating library hours.
- A student instant messages the social work librarian from a link in an online library guide.

Service Quality

Reference librarians value quality service. Today's reference librarians report that they are providing better service to their users and are successfully answering more complex questions. This belief is partially based on the ability of users to connect with a librarian using a variety of methods, such as meeting face-to-face; sending an e-mail, chat message, or text; or calling on the phone. The increased availability of digital resources to satisfy users' questions and the speed with which questions can be answered also contribute to this belief (Tenopir and Ennis 2002, 272).

Researchers are finding that the 55 percent reference rule (i.e., reference librarians answer questions correctly 55 percent of the time) may be a thing of the past in the current digital environment (Crowley and Childers 1971; Gers and Seward 1985; Hernon and McClure 1986). In a study of a university chat reference service, researchers reported questions were correctly answered 91.72 percent of the time (Arnold and Kaske 2005). The 55 percent rule was based on unobtrusive questioners and research-developed questions, whereas the 92 percent result was achieved using actual questions from real users. There remains the question of whether the accuracy criteria were comparable to those used in the 55 percent rule stream of research, but Arnold and Kaske suggest that service quality, in this one modality, is superior.

Job Satisfaction

Several studies indicate that librarians are having more fun as a result of helping users find information on the web. Academic members of the Association of Research Libraries (ARL) were surveyed four times over a decade (1991, 1995, 1997, and 2000) to measure the impact of technological changes in university reference services. The changes primarily focused on the impact of the digital resources available on the web. Reference librarians reported that they have greater job satisfaction because of technology and the greater availability of resources to answer difficult questions, and that their work has become more challenging, rewarding, and even "more fun" (Tenopir and Ennis 2001, 44).

Janes (2002) surveyed both public and academic reference librarians to determine their experiences with and attitudes toward the use of digital and networked technologies and resources in reference work. He found that librarians were both positive and optimistic about digital reference services. He reported, "Overall, then, our respondents felt that digital technologies make reference more accessible, more interesting, more challenging, and more fun. They are skeptical about their ability to make reference cheaper, but also don't think digital technologies have become more time consuming or difficult" (557).

The reality of modern libraries is that many information service needs are expected to be met 24/7 in our anywhere, anytime society. Libraries are still expected to offer traditional reference services, but now these services can reach users wherever they are, and reference librarians need to be where the users are. Users still do walk in the front door of the library, but far more often, they visit the library via the Internet.

Defining Digital Reference

Librarians continue to experiment with different reference models to meet the continually changing information landscape and to support new user demands. Reference services that are offered on the Internet are often referred to as online, digital, or virtual. There is quite a difference of opinion in the profession as just what to call these services. RUSA uses the term "virtual":

> **Virtual reference** is reference service initiated electronically, often
> in real-time, where patrons employ computers or other Internet tech-
> nology to communicate with reference staff, without being physically
> present. Communication channels used frequently in virtual reference
> include chat, videoconferencing, Voice over IP, co-browsing, e-mail,
> and instant messaging. (RUSA 2004b; emphasis added)

Both Joseph Janes (2003), founder of the Internet Public Library, and R. David Lankes (2009) use the term "digital," and M. Kathleen Kern (2008), one of the authors of the RUSA definition, uses "virtual." Andrew Pace (2003) provides an interesting perspective:

> Well, in the first place, and most simply, there is nothing virtual about
> it! You've got real patrons on one end asking questions, and real librar-
> ians (mostly) on the other end answering them. In between you have
> real questions, real answers, and a real cost of transacting both. . . .
> The very notion of virtuality—something less than real—diminishes
> the reality of hard work, new paradigms, and the shifting set of skills
> required to do the job of librarianship. (55)

Googling the terms "digital reference services" (20,800 entries) and "virtual reference services" (26,500 entries) in September 2014 to see how often each term has been used showed that "virtual reference services" was more commonly used. "Online reference services" produced 825,000 entries, but that terminology has been around for quite some time. There simply is no consensus on which term is best.

The driving force behind implementing digital reference services was the Internet. E-mail reference, the first manifestation, was the natural result of having a library webpage. In the early days of the World Wide Web, users found that little link at the very bottom of each library webpage labeled "Website Feedback" and began to use it to ask reference questions. Librarians, recognizing a need, were quick to respond by launching formal e-mail reference services. The principal users of these services were the library's primary clientele, although visitors would often request specific information about a library's unique resources. Fluctuations in use of digital reference services over time can be attributed to a number of factors, including the addition of other digital reference services such as chat or instant messaging. Easier-to-use library webpages with better-organized content and a greater availability of information on the web that quickly satisfies users' needs have also impacted this type of service.

The kinds of digital reference services offered vary among types of institutions and libraries. Many libraries have instituted some type of e-mail reference service. Other libraries offer chat reference, instant messaging, texting, or a combination of services to reach their primary user groups and to be where their users are. These services offer library users the convenience of asking questions from anywhere in the world, at any time. If the library is closed or users are not able to get to the library, they can, and do, still ask questions. An e-mail reference service is just one way to get the librarian to the user and the user to the librarian. Users are now accustomed to accessing the web 24/7, so why not the library? Of course, the reality is that librarians are not always answering the questions 24/7.

Two collaborative services do offer 24/7 availability: QuestionPoint and ipl2. QuestionPoint (www.questionpoint.org), a collaborative project of the Library of Congress (LC) and OCLC, is a cooperative comprising 1,400 libraries around the world that offers both chat and e-mail reference services 24 hours a day, 7 days a week, 365 days a year. When this project was piloted by LC in 2000 as the Collaborative Digital Reference Service, the initial intent was to "provide unprecedented access to global resources, create an archive of questions and answers as a resource for its members, and generally, add value to information on the Internet, enable 24/7 service, and redefine the role of librarian in the Internet Age" (LC 2014). The ipl2 (www.ipl.org), formerly known as the Internet Public Library, originated from a 1995 seminar taught by Dr. Joseph Janes at the University of Michigan School of Information. Today the ipl2 is hosted by Drexel University's College of Information Science and Technology and is run by a consortium of colleges and universities with graduate programs in information science. This is a 24/7, real-time, e-mail-based reference service.

Academic librarians have experimented with embedded librarians who create outposts in student centers and academic departments or through courseware, blogs, or Twitter (Kesselman and Watstein 2009), and public libraries have been moving to local shopping malls (ALA 2010). Other innovative solutions to the "go where the user is" movement include using social networking tools such as Facebook, MySpace, Ning, Twitter, and Google+ to create new online relationships with users. Since a large number of library users spend a great deal of time using social networking sites, librarians need to have a presence there to market their services. Before creating such a service, Rimland (2011) suggests reviewing the guidelines for remote access in RUSA's (2004a) "Guidelines for the Behavioral Performance of Reference and Information Service Providers" before creating a social networking campaign. The 2004 guidelines were revised in 2011; although the revised guidelines do not specifically address social networking tools, they do provide "guidelines that are specific to reference encounters where traditional visual and non-verbal cues do not exist" (RUSA 2013).

Impact of Digital Formats

Reference Resources

Just as the variety of services provided by reference librarians has changed, so too have the resources they use to answer questions. Today, reference librarians are using more digital resources than paper-based resources. The reference tools librarians use are faster, more comprehensive, and more current. Tyckoson (2011a) reflected, "When computing power was applied to information resources, our reliance on print reference sources was profoundly shaken" (223).

The use of older paper-based collections has declined as users demand and expect access to digital content. In the predigital world, paper-based indexes and abstracts, such as *Chemical Abstracts, Biological Abstracts,* the *New York Times,* and *Readers' Guide to Periodical Literature,* took up massive physical spaces in reference departments. The physical size of paper-based reference collections stored on familiar index tables and in the stacks has been reduced and replaced with tables laden with networked computers used to access the web. In a webinar on reference collections for the Association for Library Collections and Technical Services (ALCTS), Tyckoson (2010) observed that "Today's reference collections were built for librarians not users."

Reference team members at Stetson University analyzed their use of print versus electronic resources to answer reference questions. Results demonstrated that their librarians used online resources 58.54 percent of the time. The most heavily used resources were databases, the library catalog, and internally developed webpages. Printed reference books were consulted only 9.38 percent of the time (Bradford, Costello, and Lenholt 2005).

There are associated economic consequences of this conversion to digital information. An institution must continually invest in appropriate hardware infrastructure if users are to access these resources. Today, a larger proportion of a library's reference budget is spent on digital reference products—so much so that in many academic libraries, funds have shifted from the reference departments to the library's overall collections budget to support the seemingly astronomical costs associated with digital reference products with full-text content.

As more content becomes digitized, reference librarians are forced to decide whether they will replace and repurchase and, thus, duplicate large paper-based and film-based products with the expensive digital equivalents. Advantages such as increased accessibility and full-text searching capabilities offered by the digital format often provide a compelling added-value incentive.

In their decade-long study of the impact of technology on reference librarians, Carol Tenopir and Lisa A. Ennis (2001) observed, "Domination of the web as a delivery format and a portal to resources has created almost a calming effect as libraries can concentrate their efforts on a dominant format that is now familiar to most users and staff" (44–45). They concluded that "[t]o the reference librarian of the new millennium, electronic resources and services are just now the expected way of life" (45).

Instruction

Reference librarians provide different types of instruction based on the type of library in which they work. Librarians participate in formal instruction programs, which in academic libraries are often in group settings usually associated with a specific course, discipline, or assignment. Librarians also provide individual point-of-use instruction as they help users with their specific information needs. In each case, the librarian is communicating directly with the user.

Instruction delivery methods have changed as instruction found its way to the web. Today, librarians develop web-based tutorials, webinars, and library instruction modules in subject courses and offer online credit courses on information-seeking techniques. They produce YouTube videos, record podcasts, write blogs, and offer chat reference services as a means to instruct users and stay connected at the point of need. Librarians create user guides in anticipation of user needs, which Smith (2009) defines as indirect instruction.

These guides offer library users information on how to use the library's services and resources. Recently, librarians (as well as academic faculty) have begun providing worldwide access to their subject research guides by using the LibGuides portal (www.springshare.com/libguides).

The focus of instruction classes has been modified to keep up with the advances in technology, the acquisition of digital resources, and the information explosion brought about by the web. Tenopir (1999) observed that "the sheer numbers of databases and online search methods and a fast-paced rate of change have made instruction more important than ever" (278). Before the introduction of computers, library instruction often included a tour of the library and an introduction to general library policies. Library users were shown how to find books using a card catalog and where to locate the books they identified. They were introduced to print subject indexes and abstracting services to identify relevant articles on their specific topics.

In the early days of PCs, librarians found themselves teaching both the technical features of the hardware and the resources available on the web. They taught users how to use a mouse; how to find unfamiliar keys on the keyboard, such as tildes, slashes, and the enter key; and how to issue print commands. The change from paper-based to digital resources brought about the need to instruct users on both common and idiosyncratic database features and operational command structures, such as Boolean logic and relevancy. As users became more comfortable with computers and software became easier to use, the need for technical instruction decreased.

The greatest challenge for today's library users is how to harness the explosive amount of information available to them and how to identify and select the right resources for their needs. Library instruction now focuses more on the development of effective search strategies, the characteristics of different user interfaces, and the availability of unique resources. Instruction incorporates the identification and selection of appropriate disciplinary resources as well as methods to evaluate the authority, reliability, and accuracy of the information found on the web. Librarians are teaching users not only how to find information but also how to organize that information by providing instruction in the use of online bibliographic management tools, such as RefWorks, EndNote, and Zotero. These systems help researchers create databases of resources that can be used to generate bibliographies in a variety of standard formats. Instruction is often offered in specially equipped, electronic classrooms for hands-on practice.

Information Seekers

The major changes in reference work today have been driven by changes in media formats, storage capacity, computing, and the development of specialized bibliographic tools. Digitization of content has revolutionized how librarians create, store, retrieve, and preserve information. The massive amount of information available on the web has transformed how people search for information.

Since the advent of computers, the general public has believed that you can find everything you want by using a computer. At no time in history has this been as possible as it is today. Now people expect to be able to find everything they want on the web for free by simply Googling it. Conversely, librarians do not believe people always find the necessary information to fully satisfy their needs.

Today, library users no longer need to visit a library to use and/or find library resources. They are able to visit a library on the web, from anywhere in the world, at any time. Today, library users can consult the library's online catalog to determine whether the library owns an item; search a multitude of databases to identify topical research information; gain instant access to full-text articles; stream video content; analyze data files; read an e-book; organize their research using online bibliographic management tools; chat, text, IM, e-mail, Twitter, Skype, or use their mobile devices to reach a librarian. Reference librarians, too, can now provide library services from anywhere in the world. They can work from home, from their office, while they are attending a conference, or even while taking a break at the local Starbucks. Librarians using current technology can be anywhere, at any time, trying to meet the information needs of their inquiring users.

That people need help to find the information they seek has been a continuing theme in librarianship. In 1876, Samuel Swett Green, the father of reference services, pointed out, "Persons who use a popular library for purposes of investigation generally need a great deal of assistance" (74). Margaret Steig, in 1990, following a decade of availability of personal computers and at the dawn of the World Wide Web, alleged, "Few scholars, professionals, or average citizens care to acquire the expertise necessary to solve their own information needs; they did not before the library was automated, and they do not now.... Most users still need personalized guidance" (49). More recently, Linda C. Smith (2009), in her comprehensive article on reference services in the most recent edition of the *Encyclopedia of Library and Information Sciences*, proclaimed, "Reference services continue to exist in libraries because the many means of access to and use of information resources are not intuitively self-evident" (4485).

The World Wide Web turned twenty-five on March 12, 2014. The Pew Research Center's Internet and American Life Project has documented the adoption of the Internet and its impact on American life since 1995. According to a February 2014 Pew report, 87 percent of adult Americans now use the Internet and many believe it is essential to them (Fox and Rainie 2014).

In February 2012, a Pew study on search engines found that 73 percent of all Americans use search engines to find information and 91 percent of search engine users report that they usually find the information they are seeking (Purcell, Brenner, and Rainie 2012). Americans are now using the Internet for many of the same reasons that they previously used libraries—and library use has consequently changed.

In the late 1990s and early 2000s, reference librarians and library educators expressed anxiety about the reported decline in reference transactions. They were concerned about the implications for the future of reference services. There has been a great deal of speculation within the profession about the factors contributing to this decline. Some argue that the physical library will disappear. Others attribute the decline to a change in library users' information-seeking behaviors (Applegate 2008). In a survey of ARL member libraries in 2002, Novotny found that many librarians "lacked confidence in their data collection techniques" and believed that "reference service data does not accurately record their own level of activity" (12). One explanation of the decline was the movement of reference activities away from the traditional reference desk to other reference formats, such as e-mail or chat. Another explanation was that questions were becoming more difficult (Kyrillidou 2000).

Library users are now connecting with the library in different ways. They visit the library's online catalogs and access the library's indexes and databases on the web. They use library research resources such as LibGuides to find specialized disciplinary information. They find general library information, such as hours and policies, on library-created webpages. Ask any librarian today and he or she will report being busier than ever. With the explosion of information available on the web, the nature of reference questions has changed. They are often more complex and difficult and take longer to answer. Users no longer need to consult a reference librarian for simple questions that can be easily answered using their favorite search engine. Users find information on the web on their own, as is reported in the Pew surveys. They are often happy, and for the most part satisfied, when they select the top few hits from Google or Bing or check out their topic in *Wikipedia*. Smith (2009) pointed out, "In the past, reference librarians did more ready reference simply because the sources required to answer such questions were in library collections and not available to users" (4487). Today, this type of information is easily discoverable on the web.

User expectations regarding available information have also resulted in more difficult questions. Users who now consult librarians have often already checked the web and even searched some library resources. Seeking help may seem to them to be a desperate measure or possibly a last resort. Thus, users consult librarians when they cannot find the answers to their questions independently.

Not only are the questions more difficult and complex, but now there are many more places to look and resources to search to find the answers. While retrieval time itself may be shortened, searching a multitude of sources may take more time. Librarians seek to identify the best resource to satisfy a user's information needs and today that takes more time.

There has been a natural maturation in users' technological skills. Technical support questions have become more advanced as the population has developed greater computer competencies. People know more about technology; therefore, they can ask more complex questions about technology. Users in general are now more competent in the use of computers and searching the web. This increased competence can create overconfidence as well as foster a reluctance to seek assistance. It can also create great frustration when the information sought eludes discovery.

Today, users expect to find information on the web, but they are often confused by the many options confronting them. Even though they have developed relatively sophisticated web-searching skills, users may be unaware of relevant resources available and may be uncertain as to whether a specific resource is appropriate for their current need. Their access to value-added resources is often very limited if they do not use library portals. They must critically evaluate the information they find. According to one respondent in the Tenopir and Ennis (2001) study, "Gone are the days of a majority of the undergrads not having used a computer before, so computer literacy has increased, but information literacy has not in reality; although many students try to fake it, they still have very few ideas about how information is organized" (45).

The availability of digital resources has brought about significant changes in the attitudes and expectations of both reference librarians and users. Tenopir and Ennis (2002) reported, "Now both groups believe that an answer to almost every question can be found if the right combination of resources and search strategies is chosen from the multitude of web resources and online services accessible" (264).

Conclusion: Revolution or Evolution?

Reference service is an example of what Alvin Toffler (1970) called future shock. Over the past few decades, both librarians and library users have been challenged by the changes in reference resources and services. But for all of that change, the premise of reference service has held constant. Reference librarians continue to provide the link between users and the information they seek. What has really changed? Library users are more dispersed, sometimes thousands of miles away. Reference librarians need to develop fluent communication skills using multiple media. Library resources, typically available on a number of platforms, are more accessible and flexible. The questions reference librarians receive are more challenging. Answering those questions is more rewarding. The public does not always recognize that they need assistance in locating and using information. Helping library users become more capable information seekers who understand the complex realities of the information creation, distribution, organization, and use cycle remains a challenge, as it has always been.

REFERENCES

ALA (American Library Association). 2010. "Public Library in Shopping Mall." Last modified August 26. http://wikis.ala.org/professionaltips/index.php?title=Public _Library_in_Shopping_Mall.

Applegate, Rachael. 2008. "Whose Decline? Which Academic Libraries Are 'Deserted' in Terms of Reference Transactions?" *Reference and User Services Quarterly* 48 (2): 176–89. http://rusa.metapress.com/content/tx16819743420h22/fulltext.pdf.

Arnold, Julie, and Neal Kaske. 2005. "Evaluating the Quality of a Chat Service." *portal: Libraries and the Academy* 5 (2): 77–193. doi:10.1353/pla.2005.0017.

Bradford, Jane T., Barbara Costello, and Robert Lenholt. 2005. "Reference Service in the Digital Age: An Analysis of Sources Used to Answer Reference Questions." *Journal of Academic Librarianship* 31 (3): 263–72. doi:10.1016/j.acalib.2005.03.001.

Crowley, Terence, and Thomas Childers. 1971. *Information Service in Public Libraries: Two Studies.* Metuchen, NJ: Scarecrow.

Fox, Susannah, and Lee Rainie. 2014. "The Web at 25 in the U.S." Pew Research Center, Internet and American Life Project. February 27. www.pewinternet.org/2014/02/27/the-web-at-25-in-the-u-s/.

Gers, Ralph, and Lillie J. Seward. 1985. "Improving Reference Performance: Results of a Statewide Study." *Library Journal* 110 (18): 32–35.

Green, Samuel Swett 1876. "Personal Relations between Librarians and Readers." *Library Journal* 1: 74–81. http://polaris.gseis.ucla.edu/jrichardson/DIS245/personal.htm.

Hayes, Robert M. 2009. "Library Automation: History." In *Encyclopedia of Library and Information Sciences,* 3rd ed., edited by Marcia Bates and Mary Niles Maack, 3326–7. New York: Taylor and Francis. doi:10.1081/E-ELIS3–120044024.

Hernon, Peter, and Charles R. McClure. 1986. "Unobtrusive Reference Testing: The 55 Percent Rule." *Library Journal* 111 (7): 37–41.

Janes, Joseph. 2002. "Digital Reference: Reference Librarians' Experiences and Attitudes." *Journal of the American Society for Information Science and Technology* 53 (7): 549–66.

———. 2003. *Introduction to Reference Work in the Digital Age.* New York: Neal-Schuman.

Kern, M. Kathleen. 2008. *Virtual Reference Best Practice.* Chicago: American Library Association.

Kesselman, Martin A., and Sarah Barbara Watstein. 2009. "Creating Opportunities: Embedded Librarians." *Journal of Library Administration* 49 (4): 383–40. doi:10.1080/01930820902832538.

Kyrillidou, Martha. 2000. "Research Library Trends: ARL Statistics." *Journal of Academic Librarianship* 26 (6): 427–36.

Lankes, R. David. 2009. *New Concepts in Digital Reference. Synthesis Lectures on Information Concepts, Retrieval, and Services,* no. 1. San Rafael, CA: Morgan and Claypool.

LC (Library of Congress). 2014. "The Library of Congress Global Reference Network: Project History." Accessed September 8. www.loc.gov/rr/digiref/history.html.

Maxwell, Robert L. 2009. "Bibliographic Control." In *Encyclopedia of Library and Information Sciences,* 3rd ed., edited by Marcia Bates and Mary Niles Maack, 497–505. New York: Taylor and Francis. doi:10.1081/E-ELIS3-120043092.

Novotny, Eric. 2002. *Reference Service Statistics and Assessment. SPEC Kit 268.* Washington, DC: Association of Research Libraries, Office of Leadership and Management Services.

Pace, Andrew K. 2003. "Virtual Reference: What's in a Name?" *Computers in Libraries* 23 (4): 55–56.

Purcell, Kristen, Joanna Brenner, and Lee Rainie. 2012. "Search Engine Use 2012." Pew Research Center, Internet and American Life Project. March 9. www.pewinternet .org/2012/03/09/search-engine-use-2012/.

Rettig, James. 2006. "Reference Service: From Certainty to Uncertainty." *Advances in Librarianship* 30: 105–43. doi:10.1016/S0065-2830(06)30003-7.

Rimland, Emily. 2011. "Using Online Social Networking Tools for Reference and Outreach." In *Reference Reborn: Breathing New Life into Public Services Librarianship,* edited by Diane Zabel, 193–202. Santa Barbara, CA: Libraries Unlimited.

RUSA (Reference and User Services Association). 2004a. "Guidelines for Behavioral Performance of Reference and Information Service Providers." American Library Association. Approved June. www.ala.org/rusa/resources/guidelines/ guidelinesbehavioral.

———. 2004b. "Guidelines for Implementing and Maintaining Virtual Reference Services." American Library Association. Approved June. www.ala.org/rusa/resources/ guidelines/virtrefguidelines.

———. 2008. "Definitions of Reference." American Library Association. Approved January 14. www.ala.org/rusa/resources/guidelines/definitionsreference.

———. 2010. "Redefining Reference." *RUSA News,* July 1. http://rusa.ala.org/ blog/2010/07/01/redefining-reference.

———. 2013. "Guidelines for Behavioral Performance of Reference and Information Service Providers." American Library Association. Approved May 28. www.ala .org/rusa/resources/guidelines/guidelinesbehavioral.

Smith, Linda C. 2009. "Reference Services." In *Encyclopedia of Library and Information Sciences,* 3rd ed., edited by Marcia Bates and Mary Niles Maack, 4485–91. New York: Taylor and Francis. doi:10.1081/E-ELIS3-120043490.

Steig, Margaret. 1990. "Technology and the Concept of Reference, or What Will Happen to the Milkman's Cow?" *Library Journal* 115 (7): 45–9.

Tenopir, Carol. 1999. "Electronic Reference and Reference Librarians: A Look through the 1990s." *Reference Services Review* 27 (3): 276–9.

Tenopir, Carol, and Lisa A. Ennis. 2001. "Reference Services in the New Millennium." *Online* 25 (4): 40–45.

———. 2002. "A Decade of Digital Reference: 1991–2001." *Reference and User Services Quarterly* 41 (3): 264–73.

Toffler, Alvin. 1970. *Future Shock*. New York: Random House.

Tyckoson, David. 2010. "The Rise and Fall of Reference Collections: Strategies for Change." ALCTS (Association for Library Collections and Technical Services) Webcast. Originally presented April 14. www.ala.org/ala/mgrps/divs/alcts/confevents/upcoming/webinar/coll/041410refcoll.cfm.

———. 2011a. "From Print to E-Reference." In *Reference Reborn: Breathing New Life into Public Services Librarianship*, edited by Diane Zabel, 217–36. Santa Barbara, CA: Libraries Unlimited.

———. 2011b. "History and Functions of Reference Service." In *Reference and Information Services: An Introduction*, 4th ed., edited by Richard E. Bopp and Linda C. Smith, 3–22. Denver, CO: Libraries Unlimited.

Part II

REFERENCE 2.0

4

Reference Service Trends and Forecasts for Academic Librarianship

Gary Golden

T his chapter attempts, first, to provide an overview of the current state of reference and instruction in academic libraries and, second, to project a path for the delivery of those services in the immediate future. This discussion is situated within a broader framework of the state of higher education in the United States. Special consideration is paid to the financing of higher education since this is, arguably, one of the most significant challenges facing colleges and universities at the start of the twenty-first century. Finally, the chapter examines future trends and innovations that are on the horizon.

The current era represents a crucible for change in methods of delivery for reference and instructional services but also for the very nature of librarianship and the role of the information professional. A 1979 article by F. W. Lancaster and Linda Smith (1979), two University of Kentucky faculty members, predicted that it was "only a matter of time before the entire communication cycle operates in a largely electronic mode" (384). At the time of this 1979 publication, universities and librarians were in a total print environment, where communication was static and involved filling in a form, writing a letter, picking up the telephone, or going to an office or library to seek help at a service counter or reference desk. Fast-forward through the past three decades to the present day; communication is more dynamic and interactive in real time. E-mail, chats, Twitter, desktop and handheld video, blogs, and smart phones have significantly impacted administrative, teaching, and library functions at all universities. This environment sets the stage for an investigation of the academy and public service librarians. This discussion begins with the current state of academic libraries within this new environment.

The State of Academic Libraries

As members of a service organization that comes into contact with consumers on a daily basis, librarians are deeply concerned about delivering the best services to everyone at all times. They staff desks for walk-ins and use social networking tools such as e-mail, Twitter, chat, FAQs (frequently asked questions), interactive webpages, and Facebook. Since the inception of reference services, public service librarians have attempted to become integral partners with teaching faculty. The goal has been, and continues to be, to have information literacy as a component of every course. The remaining pages of this section look at some current and future trends affecting both the delivery and usage of all services in academic libraries.

Handhelds and Mobile Computing

Walking around any university campus, it is easy to see the tremendous growth in the usage of laptops, smart phones, and tablets. Kendrick (2010) reported that desktop makers would ship 291 million units annually by 2014, while makers of mobile computers, notebooks, netbooks, and tablets would ship over 400 million units by 2014. He also saw tablets growing by over 123 percent between 2011 and 2014. These devices have outstanding graphics, video and camera capabilities, and countless apps for both productivity and entertainment.

Nagy (2011), writing for a website called Business Insider, offered a very interesting take on the rapid rise of mobile computing. He stated that "round one" in mobile computing was better devices. The next "round" he saw as mobile applications, and "round three," information and how it is accessed, shared, protected, and inputted. He further saw the problem of storage being resolved by cloud technology. Consumers would be able to re-create their desktop and PC (personal computer) stored data and access it on the go. Security would be addressed, so that storage of personal records could be accomplished. Finally, Nagy reported that according to a study by Gartner, more people would be getting on the web from mobile phones than from desktop PCs by 2013. This would enable access everywhere at all times (Nagy 2011). O'Toole (2014), using January 2014 data, found that 55 percent of Internet app usage originated from smart phones and tablets. This is the first time that app usage was greater than desktop usage (O'Toole 2014). The desktop PC is not obsolete but is slowly heading toward the technology junkyard. The exponential growth of the use of mobile computing devices and the plethora of apps available afford opportunities for businesses and libraries to develop programs for consumers and patrons to handle more services on their own.

Self-Service and Ubiquitous Access

Businesses throughout the world are moving at a rapid pace toward self-service. Examples of this shift can be found in banking, gasoline stations, self-checkout at retail stores, electronic voting, vending machines, and airport kiosks. The Internet offers opportunities for self-services in retail e-commerce, professional services, online banking, e-learning, and ticketing and reservations. Include self-service utilizing smart phones, smart cards, and the telephone, and it is reasonable to assume that, throughout the world, most people participate in some type of self-service (Castro, Atkinson, and Ezell, 2010). This is true with regard to library services as well. Patrons using a computer, tablet, or smart phone can search hundreds of databases and access tens of thousands of full-text journals, newspapers, and books without the assistance of library staff. Access to electronic media and electronic reserves is 24/7. Patrons can check out and renew books, request interlibrary loan, and ask questions of a reference librarian—all in an online environment.

To assist students and faculty, academic librarians produce online tutorials and other instructional resources. Well-designed FAQs can quickly and easily answer everything from basic to more detailed questions. Libraries have seemingly embraced the concept of self-service, producing guides and webpages to facilitate remote access to databases. They offer information literacy classes to allow students to do research from a remote location and perform self-checkout and return of materials. Patrons are empowered with around-the-clock access to resources; typically they are free to access vast stores of material without the need for one-on-one help or a trip to the physical library. A report on self-service in British academic libraries found that the twenty-six respondents offered hours that they called "self-service only hours" during the days, nights, and even weekends (Jones 2004, 50–51). Services like reference, checkout, and so on, are available without any library assistance. In addition, the shift to self-service allows reference departments some flexibility in the type of staff and at what time of the day or night. This is especially important in this era of budgetary constraints.

The processes of developing self-services apps and implementing software programs that allow function without human intervention are not without financial cost. Add to development and implementation the cost of IT staff, data security, hardware, and maintenance, and clearly online self-services are not free to the organization. The primary reason for a business to implement self-services is to reduce the cost of staffing while secondarily improving the quality of support. In the case of academic libraries, the primary reason for self-services is to empower the users who want to do research from remote locations. The demographics of a changing student population show that they expect such flexibility.

Changing Student Demographics

Current student demographics are tempered by the fact that there is still a digital divide. According to 2009 Census Bureau statistics, only 31 percent of households earning less than $15,000 and only 41 percent of households earning between $15,000 and $24,999 have broadband access in the home. Another striking statistic is that almost 51 percent of households earning less than $15,000 and almost 41 percent of households earning between $15,000 and $24,999 do not use the Internet from any location. Just over 93 percent of households earning $100,000 to $149,000 and 95 percent of households earning over $150,000 have broadband access in the home. In addition, less than 4 percent of households earning over $100,000 do not use the Internet from any location (U.S. Census Bureau, 2011). Most universities provide computing equipment throughout campus for student use. However, the fact that these low-income students do not have Internet access at home and tend not to use it at all puts them at a disadvantage when they are starting their degree programs. From a public services perspective, educators cannot assume that all students know the basics about using a PC for research, writing, social networking, and search strategies.

Current student demographics and educational needs are two important factors affecting the learning and graduation success of today's student. Academic librarians need to be aware of these factors as they prepare methodologies for teaching research techniques. For example, information literacy programs must be designed to meet the expectations of the large group of nontraditional students. To design successful interactive literacy modules for the Internet, librarians need to be acutely aware of the limited time that nontraditional students spend on assignments. Librarians must design instructive but entertaining interactive webpages. Core curricula or general education classes had historically been a way to introduce students to information literacy. However, with the slow demise of these classes, librarians must find other ways to advance information literacy in partnership with teaching faculty.

The educational demographic indicators regarding student success are numerous and varied. Some indicators of student success are high graduation rates, fewer required remedial courses and general education or core courses, more hours spent on study and assignments, and career employment after graduation. A research paper titled "Time Is the Enemy" by Complete College America (2011) presented a clear representation of a student's progress toward graduation. Complete College America is a national nonprofit whose goal is to raise college graduation rates. The paper stated that 75 percent of current students on college campuses are nontraditional; that is, they were juggling jobs, families, and school. The other 25 percent attended full-time at residential colleges. Only 60 percent of full-time students and 24 percent of part-time students completed the requirements for an undergraduate degree. Full-timers took 4.7 years and part-timers took 5.6 years on average to earn a degree. Extending the data for obtaining a degree to eight years showed only a very small improvement in graduation rates (60.6 percent for full-time and 24.3 for part-time). In addition, 20.7 percent of students seeking a bachelor's degree required remedial noncredit courses. Since these were noncredit classes, taking one or more of these courses added to the time spent working toward a degree. In fact, only 35 percent of the students who took remedial courses graduated within six years (Complete College America 2011).

The book *Academically Adrift: Limited Learning on College Campuses* focuses on the significant problems in the level of learning by American students (Arum and Roksa 2011). As measured by the Collegiate Learning Assessment, 45 percent of the students in their sample did not demonstrate any score improvement in critical thinking, writing, and complex reasoning after their second year in college. In addition, 6 percent of students in highly selective colleges, 29 percent in selective colleges, and 36 percent at less selective colleges did not take a course requiring a minimum of forty pages of reading per week or a writing assignment of more than twenty pages. The authors found that the average time studying per week was twenty-five hours in 1961, twenty hours in 1981, and only thirteen hours in 2003. Only one in five students reported devoting more than twenty hours per week to studying in 2010. When hiring a new employee, 90 percent of employers rated written communication, critical thinking, and problem solving as very important for job success (Arum and Roksa 2011). A more detailed analysis of the struggles of college graduates in 2009 reported that 14 percent were unemployed or looking for full-time work. Their median salary was $30,000, and, more important, 50 percent were underemployed, working in jobs that did not require a BA or BS (John J. Heldrich Center for Workforce Development 2011).

The Teaching Faculty

The funding issues outlined earlier have also had considerable impact on the composition of the teaching faculty at institutions of higher education. An understanding of this change provides a useful framework for librarians and information professionals as they seek increased collaboration. The State Higher Education Executive Officers (SHEEO 2010) issued a report about staffing trends from 2001 to 2009 in public universities. By including the year 2009, the report captured data from the beginning of the "great recession" of 2008. SHEEO found that the most significant change in staffing in all Carnegie Classifications was the movement away from full-time tenure track faculty (a decrease of 9 percent during this period) to part-time or adjunct faculty (an increase of 2 percent). The 2010 annual report of the American Association of University Professors (AAUP 2011) noted the dramatic shift from full-time tenure track faculty to what they call contingent faculty, part-time or full-time faculty in nontenured positions. Graduate student employees and faculty members serving in contingent appointments constituted more than 75 percent of university total instructional staff. In addition, between 1975 and 2009 the numbers of contingent faculty increased by 280 percent. As a comparison, between 2007 and 2009, there was an overall 12 percent increase in college enrollment (AAUP 2011).

Having a majority of faculty as contingents presents problems for reference or instruction librarians trying to integrate information literacy into a course. Bergmann, in her 2011 dissertation, reported that adjuncts were not

well informed about support and service systems and did not have an understanding of college and departmental policies. During thirty-five years' experience in academic reference and instruction, the author of this chapter has often found it difficult to establish lines of communication with adjuncts. Many
teach at several universities, work another job, or are doctoral candidates. To
be inclusive of all faculty and students on campus, librarians need to initiate
and maintain dialogue with all instructional staff, including, and especially,
the contingent faculty. Since they teach the majority of classes, their participation in library instruction programs is vital.

As has been demonstrated, to a large part in response to radical changes
in the financing of higher education, college and universities are being challenged by students, parents, and legislators to provide greater accountability,
transparency, and fiscal responsibility in all areas. Underlying the importance
of these challenges is the fact that while access to college has increased significantly, the number of students getting a degree has not improved (Brock
2010). It is within this environment that reference librarians must be recognized as an invaluable component in students' overall educational success. A
major initiative in academic librarianship with regard to academic success is
the promotion of the concept of information literacy.

The Association of College and Research Libraries (ACRL) defines information literacy as a set of abilities requiring individuals to recognize when
information is needed and how to locate, evaluate, and use effectively the
needed information. The standards call for incorporation of information literacy across curricula, in all programs and services, which "requires the collaborative efforts of faculty, librarians, and administrators" (ACRL 2000, 4).
In addition to the traditional roles performed by academic librarians of interacting with the students through reference and instructional services, information literacy initiatives provide platforms for greater collaboration with the
teaching faculty and integration into the teaching curricula by the act of en-
suring the integration of information literacy into every major area of study on
a campus. The importance of information literacy standards and practices as
an integrated part of the curriculum cannot be understated. Several studies,
detailed in the following paragraphs, point out the need for librarians to do
more outreach to the faculty regarding these standards.

The Ethnographic Research in Illinois Academic Libraries (ERIAL) Project studied what students actually did when they were assigned a research
project for a class assignment (Asher, Duke, and Green 2010). They found that

students had gaps in their understanding of citations and search strategies beyond Google. They did not understand search logic, nor did they know how to build a search in most databases, including Google. Students also did not realize that a librarian was able to help during the research process and, in fact, had no clear perception regarding a librarian's function. In addition, university professors often acted as gatekeepers; their recommendation that a student seek help from a librarian motivated the student do so. Another study by Alison Head in 2007 found that 87 percent of assignments gave no guidelines for using the Internet, and 73 percent did not mention using the library's website. A more troublesome statistic was that 83 percent of assignments did not mention asking for assistance from a librarian.

Ithaka S+R supported two excellent research reports on faculty and libraries. The 2006 report concluded that whereas faculty stated they valued the library, they were not dependent on the library for their research and teaching. The authors saw a continued role for librarians but stated, "There appears to be growing ambivalence about the campus library" (Housewright and Schonfeld 2008). The second study in 2010 found that less than 5 percent of faculty used the library building in 2009 to start their research (compared to just over 10 percent in 2003). It also noted that faculty research processes rarely involved face-to-face consultation with a librarian (Schonfeld and Housewright 2010).

Before turning to future-casting for academic libraries, the discussion next turns to the larger environment within which that future is taking shape.

The Ecosystem of Higher Education

Several economic and societal changes have changed the landscape of higher education, a landscape in which academic libraries figure largely. A six-year W. K. Kellogg Foundation study on changes at universities was published by the American Council on Education in 1999 (Eckel et al. 1999). The authors concluded that, like most social organizations, universities are change adverse. In addition, they saw change as an art and not a science because colleges and universities are tradition based, they have internal and external pressures from competing constituencies, and change in higher education often elicits questions that have no immediate clear answers. Many of the findings of this study are still valid. While there are growing numbers of blended and online courses, the change from primarily lecture format in a traditional classroom has been slow. In many classrooms, the academy still instructs using the 2000-year-old Socratic method of questions and answers.

According to the National Center for Education Statistics (NCES 2014a), enrollment in degree-granting institutions increased by approximately 35 percent between 2000 and 2011. In addition, over the past several decades, in order to meet the needs of this increased population, colleges and universities have raised tuition and increased fees. The rise in costs has been necessary to help mitigate continued cuts in state and federal funds. Increases in tuition and fees have historically been utilized to help a school continue existing programs or engage in new initiatives. Taking advantage of this ability to raise more money, public and private universities have increased tuition and room and board (fees are not calculated) since 2000 by over 40 percent for public institutions and 28 percent in constant 2008–2009 dollars for private institutions (NCES 2014b). However, many recent economic developments—the dot.com, real estate, and banking bubbles; the debt crisis in Europe; the "Great Recession of 2008" (with its effect on endowments and unemployment); and shrinking state and federal appropriations to universities—have significantly impacted all aspects of higher education, including funding, expenditures, programs, and utilization. There is also new impetus to assess educational outputs (e.g., employment, debt, graduation rates, etc.) to help show the value of a college degree. Since universities generally encourage input from their faculty, students, and staff, the processes of investigation and subsequent change take time.

An outcry for accountability and transparency within higher education has grown out of these broader economic and societal changes. Parents, students, and politicians from state to federal levels are demanding to know how their input of dollars affects student learning, graduation rates, and postgraduate employment. In addition, they have raised concerns regarding faculty productivity, rapidly rising tuition and fees, cumbersome student debt burdens, increased use and overall impact of adjuncts, and duplicative degree programs. In their sixth annual report on student debt and employment after graduation, the Project on Student Debt (2011) reported a 5 percent increase in average debt to $25,250 and an unemployment rate of 9.1 in 2010. After spending tens of thousands of dollars and amassing a large education debt, the degree recipient expects that he or she can get a job and be a productive citizen. While education for its own sake was valued in our society in the past, today's educational goals have shifted to an economic reward focus.

State appropriations per full-time equivalent (FTE) student for all colleges in constant dollars went from $6,662 in FY2005 to $6,451 in FY2010. The five-year change FY2005 to FY2010 was a negative 3.2 percent, while the one-year change from FY2009 to FY2010 decreased by 7.2 percent. These numbers are especially troubling since 6.4 percent of educational appropriations in FY2010 came from federal stimulus (SHEEO 2010, 25). More specific numbers for the Association of Research Libraries (ARL) members reflected that 79 percent of the 93 libraries responding expected a flat or reduced budget. In addition, fifty-three libraries gave more detailed data, showing that the maximum budget cut was 22 percent, the mean was 5 percent, and the median was 4.49 percent. In addition, the top twenty ARL institutions had their endowments shrink from just over 10 percent to 30 percent. To accommodate these decreases in budget, the ARL libraries suggested staffing changes, eliminating vacant positions, hiring freezes, staff layoffs, cuts in serials and monographs, and early retirement programs (Lowry 2010, 37).

Thus, the results of examination and analysis of academic initiatives and expenditures in this new era of accountability may have a profound effect on the type of reference services provided in the future. Reference departments, as well as other library departments, must be both accountable and transparent to justify their share of this scarce resource—funding. It is within this framework of increased scrutiny of the efficacy of higher education that the state of reference services needs to be evaluated.

The Horizon

Libraries have always been early adapters of new technology, and librarians see social networking tools like Facebook, MySpace, Twitter, Second Life, Delicious, blogs, and wikis as channels for meaningful dialogue with students on their own "turf." That students feel the need to be connected to their world at all times guarantees a large audience for these and future networking tools. The library literature is full of articles on social networking, including one by Dickson and Holley (2010). They listed several programs being implemented but also voiced several concerns, a major one being whether students are receptive to the idea of an authority figure (i.e., librarian) being a part of their social network. They also pointed out that there have been very few quantitative studies; most of the reporting is anecdotal in nature. Librarians need to be clearly aware of what is transpiring in the social networking arena and how the university expects to use social networking as a teaching tool in the future. For such tools to be successful and have a positive effect on library outcomes, more research on the impact versus opportunity costs of embracing social networking needs to be done.

Teaching information literacy or bibliographic instruction has long been assumed to be both necessary and productive. Library literacy programs are supposed to be offered across the curriculum so that a graduating student is literate in research processes. ACRL provides standards, and accrediting agencies are supposed to look at a library's program in their evaluation process. However, as stated earlier in this chapter, librarians are still battling acceptance and integration into the classroom or the curriculum in many universities. Without acceptance, it is difficult, if not impossible, to develop a successful literacy program. In an excellent report for ACRL on the value of academic libraries, Megan Oakleaf (2010) presented a possible rationale for this nonacceptance: "Although the literature of information literacy instruction and assessment is voluminous, most of the literature is sporadic, disconnected, and reveals limited snapshots of the impact of academic libraries on learning" (117). She further discussed the need for assessment management systems to direct the measures of student learning. There has always been a question regarding the value of an information literacy program taught in just one course (e.g., freshman English). One has to wonder about student retention of the material presented when they actually go to do the research. More intense work needs to be done on the assessment of all information literacy classes taught throughout the curriculum. There needs to be a spirit of continuous assessment within the library, and those programs found to be ineffective need to be modified or terminated.

To determine some of what is on the horizon for colleges, one has only to read the Pew Internet and American Life Project (2011) report *The Digital Revolution and Higher Education*, based on surveys of 1,055 college presidents and 2,142 adults. The assessment of the data revealed that the presidents saw more value in online learning than did the adults in this survey. However, they all recognized the prevalence of online teaching in colleges and believed there will be significant growth in online learning over the next ten years. The presidents also believed that there will be increasing use of digital textbooks and that the majority of students will have taken at least one online course before they graduate. More than half the presidents thought that plagiarism in student papers has increased over the past ten years, and 89 percent blamed this on increased use of the Internet. Students who take online courses can be anywhere in the world and usually have no impact on campus facilities like classrooms, dorms, in-house use of libraries, and so on. However, libraries must be aware of the need to find cost-effective methods to satisfy any of the distant learners' information needs and to develop an assessment component for those needs.

The fate of the traditional reference desk employing full-time librarians is precarious at best. The continued growth in online resources and use of new communication paradigms empowers our patrons to do research from both within and external to the library. Continuous staffing of a reference desk for a patron on campus is no longer a productive way to employ high-priced reference librarians. Rather, the continued future of a stand-alone reference desk will be dependent on using this location in new and unique ways. Just as universities are moving toward increasing the percentage of part-time teaching faculty, there will no doubt be more part-time librarians in reference departments. Remote or on-demand staffing will improve productivity and save labor costs. When a patron needs reference assistance, the librarian would be summoned to the reference desk via video hookup, cell phone, pager, or intercom. Librarians should multitask at the reference desk (i.e., work at reference e-mail or chat) while waiting for patrons. Much more emphasis will be placed on providing reference assistance solely via chat, e-mail, video, and/or interactive webpages or through services contracted via for-profit companies. The traditional reference desk must be modified to reflect this model within the very near future.

The near-term future of academic libraries and their universities will be a bumpy and pothole-filled ride. Budgetary pressures on states and universities will persist or worsen, even as we continue to pull out of the "Great Recession." Universities will be required either by legislatures or by pressure from students and parents to keep increases in tuition and fees to a minimum. Universities and their departments will have to find methods to increase productivity so that they can educate and provide services to more students for less money. In the future, in order to succeed and be able to continue to serve both the universities and their students, libraries are going to have to adapt to accommodate student demographics, economic times, and ever-changing technology.

REFERENCES

ACRL (Association of College and Research Libraries). 2000. *Information Literacy Competency Standards for Higher Education*. American Library Association. Approved January 18, 2000. www.ala.org/acrl/sites/ala.org.acrl/files/content/standards/standards.pdf.

AAUP (American Association of University Professors). 2011. *It's Not Over Yet: The Annual Report on the Economic Status of the Profession, 2010–11*. Published March–April. www.asup.org/file/2010-11-Economic-Status-Report.pdf.

Arum, Richard, and Josipa Roksa. 2011. *Academically Adrift: Limited Learning on College Campuses*. Chicago: University of Chicago Press.

Asher, Andrew, Lynda Duke, and David Green. 2010. "The ERIAL Project: Ethnographic Research in Illinois Academic Libraries." *Academic Commons*, May 17. www.academiccommons.org/2014/09/09/the-erial-project-ethnographic -research-in-illinois-academic-libraries.

Bergmann, Donna Mae. 2011. "A Study of Adjunct Faculty." PhD diss., Montana State University, Bozeman.

Brock, Thomas. 2010. "Young Adults and Higher Education: Barriers and Breakthroughs to Success." *The Future of Children* 20 (1): 109–32. http://futureofchildren.org/futureofchildren/publications/docs/20_01_06.pdf.

Castro, Daniel, Robert Atkinson, and Stephen Ezell. 2010. *Embracing the Self-Service Economy*. The Information Technology and Innovation Foundation. Published April. www.itif.org/files/2010-self-service-economy.pdf.

Complete College America. 2011. "Time Is the Enemy: The Surprising Truth about Why Today's Colleges Students Aren't Graduating and What Needs to Change." Published September. www.completecollege.org/docs/Time_Is_the_Enemy.pdf.

Dickson, Andrea, and Robert Holley. 2010. "Social Networking in Academic Libraries: The Possibilities and the Concerns." *Digital Commons@Wayne State University*. http://digitalcommons.wayne.edu/slisfrp/33/.

Eckel, Peter, Madeleine Green, Barbara Hill, and William Mallon. 1999. *On Change III: Taking Charge of Change: A Primer for Colleges and Universities*. Washington, DC: American Council on Education. www.aacu.org/summerinstitutes/hips/documents/On_ChangeIIIPoliticsofChangeTrack.pdf.

Head, Alison. 2007. "Beyond Google: How Do Students Conduct Academic Research?" *First Monday* 12 (8). http://firstmonday.org/ojs/index.php/fm/article/view/1998.

Housewright, Ross, and Roger Schonfeld. 2008. *Ithaka's 2006 Studies of Key Stakeholders in the Digital Transformation in Higher Education*. Ithaka. Published August 18. www.sr.ithaka.org/sites/default/files/reports/4.16.1.pdf.

John J. Heldrich Center for Workforce Development. 2011. "Unfulfilled Expectations: Recent College Graduates Struggle in a Troubled Economy." Media release May 18. www.heldrich.rutgers.edu/sites/default/files/content/Work_Trends_Press _Release_May_2011.pdf.

Jones, Philippa. 2004. "Self-Service in Academic Libraries: A Survey of Current Practice." *SCONUL Focus* no. 32 (November 30): 49–51.

Kendrick, James. 2010. "Stat Shot: Mobile Computing Has Won." https://gigaom.com/ 2010/09/08/stat-shot-mobile-computing-has-won-2.

Lancaster, F. W., and Linda Smith. 1979. "Science, Scholarship and the Communication of Knowledge." *Library Trends* 27: 367–88.

Lowry, Charles B. 2010. "Year 2 of the 'Great Recession': Surviving the Present by Building the Future." *Journal of Library Administration* 51 (1): 37–53.

Nagy, David. 2011. "3 Reasons Why Data Will Accelerate. The Third Boom In Mobile Computing." *Business Insider.* May 4, 2011. www.businessinsider.com/3-reasons -why-data-will-accelerate-the-third-boom-in-mobile-computing-2011-5.

NCES (National Center for Education Statistics). 2014a. "Fast Facts: Do You Have Information on Postsecondary Enrollment Rates?" Accessed September 18. http://nces.ed.gov/programs/digest/d12/tables/dt12_224.asp.

———. 2014b. "Fast Facts: Tuition Costs of Colleges and Universities?" Accessed September 18. http://nces.ed.gov/fastfacts/display.asp?id=76.

Oakleaf, Megan. 2010. *Value of Academic Libraries: A Comprehensive Research Review and Report.* Association of College and Research Libraries. www.ala.org/acrl/sites/ ala.org.acrl/files/content/issues/value/val_report.pdf.

O'Toole, James. 2014. "Mobile Apps Overtake PC Internet Usage in U.S." CNN Money. Posted February 28. http://money.cnn.com/2014/02/28/technology/mobile/ mobile-apps-internet/.

Pew Internet and American Life Project. 2011. *The Digital Revolution and Higher Education: College Presidents, Public Differ on Value of Online Learning.* Pew Research Center. August 28. www.pewsocialtrends.org/files/2011/08/ online-learning.pdf.

Project on Student Debt. 2011. *Student Debt and the Class of 2010.* Published November. http://projectonstudentdebt.org/files/pub/classof2010.pdf.

Schonfeld, Roger C., and Ross Housewright. 2010. *Faculty Survey 2009: Key Strategic Insights for Libraries, Publishers, and Societies.* Ithaka S+R. April 7. https://cyber.law.harvard.edu/communia2010/sites/communia2010/images/ Faculty_Study_2009.pdf.

SHEEO (State Higher Education Executive Officers). 2010. *State Higher Education Finance FY 2010.* www.sheeo.org/finance/shef_fy10.pdf.

5

The State of Reference in School Libraries

Lawrence V. Ghezzi and Walter Johnson

What is the state of reference in school libraries? Before this question can be addressed, others must be asked and answered: What is the definition of a "school library," and who are the individuals providing the reference services? What is a virtual library, and how can virtual libraries be used in schools? How have virtual libraries transformed today's school libraries? What roles do school librarians play within this changing learning environment? And what is the role of reference for today's school librarian?

Defining School Libraries and Librarians

In this time of transition from conventional to virtual services, it is not only the reference services that are being reshaped but also entire spaces and position descriptions. The physical changes in the spaces where students seek information affect the way reference and instruction services are delivered. The names of these physical spaces do not always identify them as libraries, with some being labeled as "media centers" or "information commons." While the term "school library" often refers to those in a K–12 environment, this chapter discusses some innovations and examples from post–secondary schools.

Just as the names of the physical spaces are not always consistent, neither is the description of the person providing the reference assistance. According to the official web log of the American Association of School Librarians (AASL), the term "school librarian" was officially adopted as the title used to describe the individual providing reference services in a school library (Pentlin 2010). Previously, the term "school library media specialist" had been the official term. In addition to the official terms, these professionals have been known as "media specialists," "teacher librarians," "library teachers," and other similar descriptive titles. The reaction to this name change has not been entirely positive, with many in the profession thinking that this change was a return to an outdated title that many states had already abandoned (Staino 2010).

The authors found no indication in the real world that school districts are following this recommendation. A perusal of several school websites, staff directories, and media center websites confirmed that this change is not universal. Colleges and universities continue to offer courses in media specialization. The authors' state of employment, New Jersey, uses the term "school library media specialist," and while the authors identify with the former term, the official AASL term, "school librarian," is used in this chapter. Regardless of the name used, professionals who maintain, manage, and are leading school libraries into the future are currently faced with many challenges involving the changing face of school library reference.

The Nature of Virtual Libraries

In the past, a library was measured by the *physical* size of the library and the *physical* numbers in its collection. Today, size is determined by the packet of the library's server. Through electronics, any library, regardless of dimension and position, can tout possession of the complete contents of the Library of Congress, the complete repository of the Louvre, the complete assemblage of the Dead Sea Scrolls, the complete aggregation of the Victoria and Albert Museum, the complete treasures of the Vatican, and so on. All of this can be available on a computer monitor or, as is fast becoming the case, on a minuscule plastic instrument attached to the belt of any person.

Although there is an extensive scope of technology available to students in different school districts, often restricted by socioeconomic factors, digital accessibility is more and more the norm rather than the exception. As a consequence, the avenue of access is no longer confined to a particular geographic position. A student may access the library's resources while sipping a Cinnamon Dolce Latte at Starbucks, curled up on a comfortable bed, or sitting under the leafy boughs of an elm tree. In addition, literally millions of sources of trivia (some of which may actually be accurate) can also be found in the blink of an eye.

What impact does this readily available pastiche of information have on a typical school library and its users? How has it changed reference in school libraries? Let us first look at the manner in which computerization and the World Wide Web have changed what typifies a library.

What Is a Virtual Library?

Surely, the word "library" needs no explanation, although it can encompass a diversity of items, such as books, maps, sound or video recordings, and the like. Its chief attribute is that it is physical. The word "virtual" is defined by *Webster's New Collegiate Dictionary* as "being in essence, but not in fact." Therefore, it would seem that a virtual library is one which is in essence a library but not in fact a library. This contradiction is, very often, the basis of confusion when school librarians discuss "virtual libraries."

Several definitions of a virtual library can be found via a Google search on the web. A virtual library can be:

- A library that has no physical existence, being constructed solely in electronic form.
- Access to electronic information in a variety of remote locations through a local online catalog or other gateway, such as the Internet.
- A search aid that combines Internet technology with traditional library methods of cataloging and assessing data.
- A directory that contains collections of resources that librarians or other information specialists have carefully chosen and organized in a logical way.
- An annotated, frequently updated subject guide to online resources (documents, databases, mailing lists, catalogs of links).

For the purposes of this chapter, we use the second definition—"Access to electronic information in a variety of remote locations through a local online catalog or other gateway, such as the Internet"—expanding the definition somewhat to include resources that may exist on-site or off-site utilizing Internet technology.

Do Virtual Libraries Currently Exist?

The answer is an emphatic *YES!* In the real world, every time someone logs on to the World Wide Web, that person is making use of virtual libraries, be it reading an article in the *New York Times Online*, perusing information at Weather.com, or placing an order at ShopRite. There are also other, more "conventional" virtual libraries.

The U.S. Library of Congress and the New York Public Library (NYPL), for example, have digitized huge areas of their book collections. The Elizabethtown College website (www.etown.edu) lists twenty-six virtual libraries that are searchable system-wide. The diverse list ranges from the European Commission Libraries, to the Karlsruhe (Germany) University Virtual Catalog, to the Military Education and Research Library Network, to the United Nations System Shared Cataloguing and Public Access System, to mention a few. Some major libraries listed include the National Library of Australia, the British Library, the University of Texas Libraries (which has links to online books in English and other languages), and INFOMINE (University of California) listings of databases, electronic journals, electronic books, bulletin boards, electronic discussion lists, online library card catalogs, as well as articles and directories of researchers. These listings are updated on a regular basis, making them more current than print versions.

How Does a Virtual School Library Affect Existing Collections and Librarians?

A virtual library can both enhance and supplement existing school library collections. For example, a small library may have just a few books on pre-Columbian art. Through the use of the Internet and other electronic resources, additional materials on pre-Columbian art can be made available to students, thus *supplementing* the existing collection. Taking it a step further, the library can make available electronic media on other art styles, thereby *enhancing* its collection of art resources. "In no institution does the expectation of electronic miracles make better sense than in libraries. Where, if not in these great repositories of information, positioned as they are smack-dab in the middle of the information age, on the very crossroads of all the information highways, should electronics be more useful?"(von Hoffman 1996, 130).

Longtime library employees accustomed to the traditional research methods utilizing hard-copy reference materials may feel threatened by the incursion of the Internet and other electronic resources into a library. They may think that their jobs will become unnecessary as more and more library users bypass them to acquire the information they seek. Real-world experience tends to be the opposite.

In his 1996 article on electronic libraries, von Hoffman referenced George Needham's (formerly of the Public Library Association) words that "without the staff to help people use the machines, the equipment will be 'little more than Pentium paperweights'" (130). The article went on to warn about not only the affordability of replacing hardware year to year but also being able to afford the staff needed to assist patrons with its use. Von Hoffman quoted William D. Walker, senior vice president of the Research Libraries of the NYPL: "If people are using things like the World Wide Web, we need one staff member out on the floor for every twenty workstations in use. But if people are working with statistical data packages, they need a very different level of staff person" (130). These statements, made when Google was only just beginning, remain true today. While the hardware and technology have changed, the need for librarians to assist patrons in their use has, if anything, increased with changes in technology.

Libraries must continue to consider the problems posed by future changes in technology. Educated guesses can be made about what these changes will be, but there is absolutely no certainty about what will turn out to be useful, economical, and popular. Consider, for example, the battle between the Betamax and the VHS video-recording systems a number of decades ago. Betamax was a superior recording system, but the buying public chose the less expensive, somewhat inferior VHS system because of the availability of inexpensive, prerecorded VHS videotapes.

Another advantage of virtual libraries, especially when speaking about school libraries, lies in the greater utilization of space. What once took miles of shelving can now be accessed through a laptop computer. Even if the library maintains its database on CDs, the space saving is phenomenal. For example, the entire *National Geographic Magazine* from 1888 through 1999—including articles, photographs, and advertisements—can be stored in nine inches of shelving space. Other standard reference books, for example, *Encyclopaedia Britannica*, *Bartlett's Quotations*, *World Book Encyclopedia* (multimedia version that includes video and sound), *Grolier's Encyclopedia*, and *Webster's Unabridged Dictionary* are available on single CDs. With today's online access and cloud storage, even space for CDs and DVDs is becoming less important.

How User-Friendly Are Virtual School Libraries?

Today's crop of students has grown up surrounded by computer technology; they are the so-called digital natives (Prensky 2001). Most primary school students are more familiar with the working of the World Wide Web than with the arcane method of searching through three-by-five index cards in a long oak drawer. Most websites are well designed and easily navigated. The plethora of search engines makes finding information about the most abstruse subject a simple and rapid matter of clicking away. Dr. Lawrence H. Summers (2011), President Emeritus of Harvard University, commented during his keynote address to the New York Times Schools for Tomorrow conference that he had seen a fifteen-month-old use one with some success. Doug Levin (2011), Executive Director of the State Educational Technology Directors Association, opined that "students themselves already use the technology to play games or connect with friends on Facebook."

If students themselves are already using the technology, what level of training is required for them and for staff? In most cases, little or no training is required for students. It would be the singular student of any age who would not know how to use a mouse or a keyboard. Staff, on the other hand, is entirely a different matter. Generally speaking, educators and library staff tend to be less experienced in computer literacy. They have grown up without the digital devices of today and may feel uncomfortable—even threatened—by computer technology; they are the so-called digital immigrants (Prensky 2001). In-house training and attendance at seminars and off-site classes (often conducted at regional libraries and community colleges) as well as one-on-one peer instruction are all viable avenues to elevate staff knowledge to appropriate levels.

Is a Virtual Library Simply Another Informational Tool?

A videotape is an informational tool; a VCR is a device to access the videotape (the informational tool). A virtual library is a device to access digital information, either through a digital medium or via the World Wide Web. Of itself, it is nothing, just as a library building, of itself, is not knowledge. However, the knowledge that is available through a virtual library is astounding, limitless, and unsurpassed by conventional libraries. The virtual library also is capable of being updated instantaneously, unlike conventional libraries that may lag years behind in purchasing new editions of reference books. In 2003, a survey of library books by a Parent Teacher Organization (PTO) member at a primary school in coastal New Jersey discovered a science book that stated: "While the possibility of a human landing on the moon is technically possible, it is unlikely that it will happen in this century." This was the most current science book available in that library.

As mentioned earlier, more and more of today's students—primary, secondary, and college level—are incredibly computer literate. They have grown up with computer technology and consider it as commonplace as Gen Xers would have considered VCRs. Many colleges, in fact, provide freshmen with laptops as part of the basic school package, along with books, pencils, paper, and lunch passes. In fact, today's students would be stymied by the traditional methods of research: shifting through card files, pulling out mountains of books, making notations on yellow pads, and pulling it all together on a typewriter. The philosophy of research has changed dramatically with the advent of the World Wide Web and the proliferation of inexpensive computers. Libraries and staff that attempt to maintain the status quo will be left behind.

To this end, school librarians and library staff must accept that the computer in its various configurations (laptops, e-readers, iPads, smart phones, etc.)—and random learning, as opposed to structured learning—is a valid research tool, and not just as a passing fancy of the younger generation. Many library and media centers have accepted technology as a valid learning tool for a generation raised on television and computers, and they have seen dramatic increases in resource usage.

School librarians who are willing to invest the time and energy in learning new technological skills can see a dramatic increase in students' learning skills and performance levels. The East Mooresville (North Carolina) Intermediate School utilizes MacBooks in its fifth grade math class to enable students to work their way through advanced assignments. As Mark Edwards, superintendent of Mooresville Grade School District, in a personal conversation with the author several years ago, put it, "It's not about the box. It's about changing the culture of instruction—preparing students for their future, not our past." The district's graduation rate was 91 percent in 2011, up from 80 percent in 2008. On state tests in reading, math, and science, an average of 88 percent of students across grades and subjects met proficiency standards, compared with 75 percent three years ago. Attendance is up, dropouts are down. Mooresville ranks 100th out of 115 districts in North Carolina in terms of dollars spent per student, but it is now third in test scores and second in graduation rates (Schwarz 2012).

Are There Limitations to the Technology?

While thankfully the attitude is losing ground, there are still pockets of educators who fear a reliance on computer usage: "What if the electricity fails? Nobody can use the computer." Of course, if there were a major power outage, the libraries would have to close and students would not be able to use books anyway. In addition, inexpensive battery backups are available that enable users to complete their online research without losing the information obtained. Given both of these points, such an argument is clearly baseless.

There are schools, however, that do not use technology; one such school is the Waldorf School of the Peninsula, which eschews the use of any technology in its 160 locations. The Waldorf teaching philosophy is focused on physical activity and learning through creative, hands-on tasks. It is based on the belief that computers inhibit creative thinking, movement, human interaction, and attention spans. (Interestingly, this Los Altos, California, school includes students whose parents are officers and employees of eBay, Google, Apple, Yahoo!, and Hewlett-Packard.) The classrooms' low-tech equipment includes blackboards, colored chalk, reference books, and number-2 pencils. Fractions are taught by cutting into food, which is later consumed by the students. Do the children learn any better? The Waldorf School admits it is difficult to compare since, as a private school, they do not administer standardized tests in elementary grades (Richtel 2011).

Socioeconomic Factors

Computers are everywhere, from the desktop to the smart phone. It would be difficult to find an educational environment—not to mention a place in the world at large—where computer terminals did not exist. And many of today's students, as previously mentioned, have a high degree of computer competency, much of it innate. Unfortunately, socioeconomic factors can negatively impact students from poorer environments who may not have similar competency with using digital equipment in a scholastic environment, although anecdotal evidence tends to indicate that the usage of some forms of computers (e.g., iPads, cell phones, and smart phones) is becoming less constrained by economics.

Walking through parks, streets, malls, and schools located in a variety of environments, one will see a large number of young people with cell phones.

While it may be that some cost analyses have been conducted, anecdotal evidence indicates that the multiuser aspect of computer terminals, servers, and other digital media dramatically reduces the per-user cost of research and reference materials. As an example, several thousand schools can access materials in the U.S. Library of Congress via the web; this means that those schools do not need to purchase a hard copy of a book for their stacks. Money not spent on books can be used elsewhere in the media center to enhance access to virtual library resources.

In the Matawan-Aberdeen Regional School District (Monmouth County, New Jersey), Nooks are replacing books. The district worked with Barnes & Noble to acquire fifty-four Nooks at a cost of $99 each. According to Zach Gross, the media specialist at the Matawan Regional High School, "compared with the cost of buying actual books, we are saving money in the long run. This reduces the number of books that will be lost or damaged. We won't have to worry about replacing books from wear" (Antonucci 2012, 3). Furthermore, according to Gross, they "no longer buy reference books since students have unlimited resources to that information. [Pointing to the reference section] . . . that whole area is eventually going to be replaced with digital" (Antonucci 2012, 3). Classical books required by students are available digitally and students are encouraged to use their personal devices (cell phones, iPads, and iPods) to download materials as part of the district's "Bring Your Own Device" initiative, allowing students to use their cell phones, personal laptops, and other devices during classroom instruction (Antonucci 2012).

Limited Access to Resources

Unfortunately, there is the widespread belief that one can call up all of Western civilization's writings on the computer screen, but nothing could be further from the truth. Of the millions of books on library shelves throughout the world, only a relative handful can be summoned onto the computer screen. For example, the Library of Congress has nearly 100 million items in its catalogs, but, according to the Library of Congress website (www.loc.gov), only "several million" are available digitally. Furthermore, contemporary publishers are not eager to produce digital formats for the various e-readers due to a fear of lost sales. There is much contention between publishers and libraries over this issue. Publishers are also reluctant to invest in the various e-book formats or to provide audiobooks for all titles.

Transformation: Models and Examples

Libraries are now struggling to fit electronic modules into an edifice layout that never anticipated anything other than physical collections. How, then, are modern libraries to accommodate the explosion of contemporary electronic devices and protocols that are required, indeed demanded, by today's technologically oriented student?

The physical structure of the library will have to be transformed from a warehouse of books and media into a communications command post. Flexible space will have to be provided for various activities, ranging from small group projects to individual students working in a multimedia lab or audiovisual studio. In order to empower students to communicate through a variety of modes and media, the library must have the technological capabilities necessary.

Redesigning Space and Services

There are exciting examples of how school libraries can be restructured to focus on clients, accommodate technology, provide for information skills training of clients, be cost-effective, allow for printed collections that are still growing despite shrinking expansion rates, accommodate staff whose primary activity is service to users, and support the social role the library has always played.

One example from 1999 is the University of Queensland (Australia), which designed a library with over 700 PCs (with 400 of these available for public access) serving 25,000 students and 4,800 staff and researchers (Schmidt, Croud, and Turnbull 2000). The Queensland Library used as its slogan "We link people with information." This, then, was the focus of the redesign: working in partnership with teaching departments; supporting and adding value to teaching, learning, research, and community services; and responding to current needs while anticipating and preparing for future needs (Schmidt and Wilson 1998).

Today's school libraries require on-screen computer access to resources with visual images that are stored locally or remotely. Readers like to sit or lie on the floor, with many preferring "noisy" spaces. In higher education, the learning environment emphasizes learner-centered and problem-based approaches to teaching, lifelong learning, and flexible delivery of programs. The student is now a customer with needs and wants. A successful school library or media center must use marketing approaches that emphasis the customer. In other words, the physical space and the school librarian are navigators for a client using a computer to access electronic resources. The library is a window on the world.

In redesigning the existing layout, the Queensland staff developed several flowcharts of possible activities of library users as well as an analysis of seating. Students appeared to be staying away in droves from the neatly arranged carrels, preferring to sprawl at tables and spaces closer to the collections. The media center had to be marketed as an attractive place to study, with a variety of comfortable seating arrangements for both individuals and groups; it also needed to provide a social meeting area, dial-up user access, space for library staff and client meetings, and appropriate amenities for staff.

All of the services to be provided by the library were identified, and the nature, character, clientele, and relationships with other services were described and delineated. Visits were made to other service organizations, including banks, Internet cafés, telecommunication service providers, and music/hi-fi stores, to "unfreeze" current library design perceptions and present new ideas for incorporation in the new library model. Should the new library be more like a supermarket or a shopping mall? What could be learned from service providers that had already responded flexibly to client needs?

Early discussions focused on the creation of an abstract diagram that would represent the ideal model without reference to the physical constraints of existing buildings. This was done to avoid the existing physical layouts driving the agenda rather than the client (i.e., student) needs.

It became obvious that all students do not study in the same way. Inherent in the design was a variety of study spaces reflecting the diverse needs of the students. The following were identified:

- Group study
- Noisy study
- Quiet study
- Individual study rooms
- Comfortable reading areas
- Study for people with disabilities
- Advanced study services
- Electronic study, both beginner and advanced
- Study with coffee
- Study with music

The outcome of the previous research resulted in a library that includes a "hub" where assistance is provided, training rooms, workstations, a display area for new materials, copying facilities, and a self-service checkout. Students can easily access the print collections as well as the virtual collections, either housed within the facility or off-site (off-site, of course, refers to any virtual collections anywhere in the world), and there is an information assistance desk where students can get specialized help.

A more recent example of the changing nature of post–secondary school libraries is the College of New Jersey, which recently opened its $35-million library that reflects the changing nature of college libraries. "A library is not just a warehouse for storing books. A library is a place you go to be in a library," says Tara Pavlovsky, the library dean (Heyboer 2005). Taking a cue from coffee shops and bookstores that attract students in droves, the library has plush armchairs and ottomans, big windows, soft colors, and a coffee bar. It seems more like a large bookstore than a college library.

Finding the balance between virtual and print is a delicate art. An example of a virtual library that accommodates an extensive existing print collection is the Middletown Township (New Jersey) Public Library. It is a state-of-the-art library integrating conventional and virtual collections. The main branch includes forty workstations: eight are dedicated to the library's catalog, sixteen are for adult users, four are in the Teen Room, and twelve are in the Children's Room. Card holders can access the library's catalog, request additions to the library's collection, renew books or electronic media, and reserve books or media without ever setting foot in the building. Self-checkout of books and media is accomplished via a touch terminal utilizing RFID (radio frequency identification) coding. This system also generates automatic phone calls when materials have not been returned on time. One might conjecture that this would result in fewer people visiting the physical library, but, in actuality, according to the library's annual reports, circulation has been increasing each year.

The Middletown Township Public Library reopened approximately a year ago after an extensive remodeling and expansion program, including the incorporation of many of the features described in the Queensland project. The new library has received many compliments on its appearance, functionality, and user-friendliness. The bottom line is a 77 percent increase in circulation and a dramatic increase in patronage. In fact, the library broke with its tradition and added Sunday hours to meet the needs of its users.

Many public libraries are taking a more virtual approach as technology becomes available. Audiobooks can be borrowed from the library without using CDs or audiotapes, taking car trips, or incurring late fines. The popularity of e-readers has led to a surge in demand for e-books. Libraries are offering access 24/7 and considering the needs of those too busy or too far to travel to a physical space. Vendors such as OverDrive, OCLC (Online Computer Library Center), and NetLibrary were in more than 1,000 libraries across the country in 2005 (Hill 2005), with this number increasing exponentially each year. The previously mentioned Matawan-Aberdeen Regional School District and the Mooresville School District are pilot programs that are being viewed as possible role models for digital school integration. Major obstacles to incorporating these models into existing school districts are the need to make very painful staff and technological changes to free up financial resources.

Planning for Partnerships and Collaboration

When given the opportunity to develop space and services, it is important that school libraries look to emulate what is being done in the local colleges and communities, as with the earlier examples. Along with considering these spaces as models, school librarians should be looking at them for possible partnerships. There are several examples of public and school library collaboration listed on the Association for Library Service to Children (ALSC) website (www.ala.org/alsc/schoolplcoop#campaigns). These examples include library card campaigns, increasing registration through the schools, and sometimes targeting specific classes, such as kindergarten and first grade. Assignment alerts can be set up to inform the public librarians of specific school assignments, helping those librarians assist the students. There are also examples of school librarians visiting the public libraries and public librarians going to the schools.

There have been innovative examples of conventional-virtual library integration, such as the QandANJ program, a network of experienced New Jersey librarians offering free, live, interactive search assistance 24/7, which was terminated in December 2011 due to lack of funding. With forty-four member libraries, QandANJ was supported in whole or in part by the Institute of Museum and Library Services through the Library Services and Technology Act, administered by the New Jersey State Library (an affiliate of Thomas Edison State College), managed by the South Jersey Regional Library Cooperative, and staffed by member libraries in the New Jersey Library Network. It is unfortunate that due to state budget cuts, along with this New Jersey example, other similar services from different states have also ceased. However, this cooperation between multiple library service points continues to happen in Florida through its Ask a Librarian website (www.askalibrarian.org). It is hoped that these services will continue and that others may be reinstated in the future.

There are many examples of public libraries targeting young readers that can be used as models for school libraries. Recognizing the need to encourage youngsters to become familiar with, and comfortable within, a library setting, many municipal libraries are forming partnerships with local schools to present reading programs. One national program is "Read to a Dog" (Reading Education Assistance Dogs program; www.therapyanimals.org/R.E.A.D .html). This program allows new readers to read aloud to a trained therapy dog. The Middletown Township Public Library has a monthly program at two of its branches. The high volume of attendance has required the library to take reservations for each session and limit participation to ten-minute modules.

While many acknowledge the importance of collaboration, actual implementation is not always an easy process. School librarians need to be aware of the opportunities and take advantage of them when they are available. As funding in both school and public libraries continues to dwindle, it would be beneficial for both to work toward sharing resources. While many of the examples listed on the ALSC website can be used as models, it is important that school librarians address some of the questions discussed by Tasha Squires (2009) in her book *Library Partnerships*. These questions involve finding ways to approach other libraries, developing long-term relationships, establishing connections and sharing resources, and, of course, securing the ever important funding.

Using Social Media to Educate

In the early days of cell phones, their use was condemned by educators and they were banished from classrooms. Despite this, Facebook, Twitter, online blogs, and YouTube have become a constant habit in the lives of students as well as adults. Today, rather than shunning the once-perceived obstacle to students' attention, educators across New Jersey are embracing social media as a way of engaging young people. A survey of college and higher education instructors indicated that 80 percent of nearly 2,000 faculty members polled used social media in the classroom (Oglesby 2012). The study also reported that 30 percent used social media to make material available to students outside of class. More and more teachers are using YouTube and video-streaming websites to illustrate lessons and blogs for student discussion.

In the General Management Program at the Paris business school, Essec, entering students are provided with an iPad, Facebook is used to foster a sense of community among the students, and Twitter is used to allow large groups of students to interact with lecturers. Videoconferencing is an avenue to unite students and lecturers scattered around the globe. Internally, the school relies heavily on Google for Gmail, Google+ for social networking, and Google docs for teaching materials (Schuetze 2011).

Rutgers University in New Jersey created digital extension of classrooms with blog-hosted discussions and class supplements in the form of streaming video. The use of digital communication has enabled both students and teachers to break down the boundaries of time, borders, culture, and generations.

Students use Facebook or Twitter to complete school assignments, seek assistance from instructors or peers, and check peer leadership for group discussions of projects. Many secondary and high schools now allow the use of cell phones between periods, at lunchtime, and at the request of teachers. Many teachers, as well as students, have found quick access to the Internet to be helpful. As one principal stated, "We have all these minicomputers attached to kids' hips." And a smart phone is truly a portable computer (Oglesby 2012).

Many instructors have adopted the service known as eClicker that allows students to text-message quiz answers directly to the instructors, thereby eliminating the feedback time required to grade papers. According to the description on the iTunes website (https://itunes.apple.com/us/app/eclicker-client/id329200145?mt=8), eClicker is a personal response system that allows teachers to poll their class during a lesson. It provides teachers with the real-time feedback they need to be sure their messages are being received. Features include a Wi-Fi-based classroom response system for up to sixty-four clients; student participation with any Internet-enabled device; ability to edit questions on a computer or iOS device; option to add or draw images with questions; and sharing of sets with other teachers via Bluetooth. A teacher can also poll questions one at a time or back-to-back and review historical polling data and e-mail reports. Others will blog assignments for later access by students.

At least one corporation, Pearson Learning Solutions, is looking for ways to meld social media with its products and give students online identities for web class work. According to the website (www.pearsonlearningsolutions .com), "Pearson promotes the use of technology as an educational resource in the classroom, at home, and on-the-go, and offers educational technology solutions that allow innovative technological vision to become a reality for the betterment of the learning environment at-large."

One New Jersey school district used social media to coordinate communication on a joint school project between two high schools. Students in the Morris County (New Jersey) East Hanover School District used social media to share their needs for a bench with the shop students at East Hanover Middle School. The students used Skype to oversee the construction (Oglesby 2012). Perhaps the most appealing aspect of social media is its cost. As one instructor said, "It's all free. It's all accessible" (Corbett 2012).

Smart phones and iPads are the composition notebooks of the twenty-first century, albeit the new versions come in many skins to personalize the equipment, as opposed to the standard black-and-white splatter pattern. Norma Blake, retiring New Jersey State Librarian, is looking at a pilot program to bring iPad dispensing machines to local libraries (Corbett 2012). This would be a major step forward from the sale of floppies and thumb drives that currently exists in many libraries. Many libraries have already migrated to the latest digital technology imported from Japan: QR (quick response) codes. These little squares of black-and-white boxes that can be read by smart phones immediately connect the user to the library's website, where surfing can be initiated. The Middletown Township Public Library, discussed earlier, launched just such a service in May 2012. Users are able to not only access the library's website portal but also search, reserve, and renew materials.

The School Librarian in Today's Learning Environment

As American society has transformed itself from the Industrial Age to today's Information Age, school librarians have had to redefine their roles within the framework of the school's instructional realm (Mehlinger 1996). Traditional library skills have not transmuted into information resources skills. Let us look at a generic school librarian job description that can be found online (http://careers.stateuniversity.com):

> Elementary school librarians teach basic library skills, often in regularly scheduled classes in the library. They may teach students how to distinguish among various kinds of books, such as fiction, nonfiction, poetry, and biography, and how to use the classification systems for finding books and other materials. They encourage use of the library for information and recreation, while making it an interesting

and important part of the school day. To interest students in reading, librarians may conduct story hours for the younger students and arrange special programs for those in the higher grades.

Most students begin to learn research techniques in junior and senior high school, so secondary school librarians usually hold orientation sessions for individual classes to explain the use of card catalogs, computer databases, reference books, indexes to periodicals, and audiovisual materials. They help individual students by suggesting specific sources or ways of finding information. Sometimes librarians set up exhibits designed to make students aware of library holdings, often coordinating the exhibits with historical events or holidays.

While much of this job description is applicable in a general way to today's world, some specifics are no longer relevant to today's student (e.g., using the Dewey Decimal System to find materials and how to use a card catalog). Instead, the contemporary librarian must be extremely computer literate with a level of expertise that, at the very least, matches that of the students who live in daily contact with smart phones, laptops, and iPads. The librarian must be able to navigate the superfluity of search engines (e.g., Google, Ask.com, and Bing), advise the student on the exactness of the reference, and caution the student on the dangers of plagiarism. The librarian must function as a mentor to the student in refining a search parameter to locate the precise material required. The librarian must also be intimately acquainted with the many free reference resources available online that complement the physical acquisitions housed in the library. The librarian must also be a hardware mechanic for such times as when a printer will not print (sometimes with such a simple fix as adding paper to the machine) and a software guru for those times when "The computer does not want to do anything!"

How students learn is changing, and the library must change with it. Long gone are the silent alleyways stacked with leather-bound books; the "silence" signs; the elderly woman wearing a cameo, half-glasses suspended from her neck by a small chain, with a tight bun of graying hair and a perpetual scowl on her face; and the concept that the library is a hallowed hall bordering on the sacred. Today's library is bright, open, and even noisy, as students collaborate on projects, running back and forth between work carrels and computer terminals. In the near future, the rooms may be total devoid of books and magazines as all resources become available digitally. As mentioned earlier, the four-foot-wide *Encyclopaedia Britannica* stack has been replaced by either a quarter-centimeter-thick shiny disc or a simple keystroke. Changes in a school library come about in a variety of ways. As the library moves from a facility that provides information to one that creates a center for learning, library policies have to be reexamined. A library schedule must be flexible enough to allow students access to information when the need arises from the curriculum. To accomplish this, the librarian must be a consultant to teachers on unit planning as well as equipment usage (Clark 1991). In the lead author's personal experience, the latter issue has been a serious matter.

During the past two decades, there have been many attempts to train teachers in the use of computers. Unfortunately, most of the training has focused on the use of computers as an administrative tool rather than as a teaching tool. Recent studies have indicated that a large percentage of teachers have learned to handle administrative tasks (attendance, grade reporting, e-mailing) on the computer but have not learned to use the computer as an adjunct to their teaching modalities.

How are these teachers to be taught to use computers in a pedagogical setting? Who are the best teachers of teachers? This question was raised by Merle Marsh, EdD, in an article on teacher development, particularly in the use of technologies in the classroom. According to the article, which has now been archived, "The answer most given is almost universal: other teachers." She continued: "It makes sense. Other teachers know. They are aware of the demands on time and talent. . . . Teachers recognize those who are exceptional teachers and copy them in their own way. They model what successful teachers are doing and reshape the methods to fit their unique style. . . . Nowhere is this more obvious than in learning how to use technologies and how to integrate them into the curriculum" (Marsh 2008). In other words, librarians gather skills from other teachers that they use to fortify their own methods.

Marsh (2008) makes the valid point that most schools, unlike the commercial world, do not have the luxury of hiring a staff of professionally trained computer experts to set everything up, train everyone who needs to learn how to use the technologies, keep everything running, and provide individualized help when needed. Even if they did, most of the teachers' learning would come from other teachers because computer engineers are not experts in education and the art of teaching children.

Most educators appear eager to integrate computers into their curricula. Unfortunately, computer usage has stagnated in the areas of administrative tasks simply because no one has shown the teachers how to use computers to teach.

Making Computers Earn Their Living

There are examples of librarians using innovative and creative ways to help educators realize the full potential of available technology. Ranging from discussion of a complex multiday workshop to something as simple as replacing batteries, Marsh (2008) described how librarians and educators are working to overcome technological inertia. School librarians have developed non-threatening and fun programs to encourage teacher use of the Internet, with teachers responding positively to the entertaining element of the program.

For many educators, according to Alejandro Franco (2006), utilizing computers for teaching can be a threatening experience, particularly in a virtual environment, because "interaction in virtual education is given mostly in [writing] (and we know that frequently it is a great difficulty for some teachers to write). Also, for many, to face the new course could be the problem, when he/she is already accustomed to use an easy pedagogy in which the same class is repeated semester after semester without having to make the effort of researching, of improving, of enlarging the cognitive spectrum." Franco further asserted that the educator must "transform the traditional pedagogy toward an electronic pedagogy in which the professor becomes a *facilitator* of the student's learning process and an active pedagogy supporter" (emphasis added).

Unfortunately, school administrators commonly exacerbate the situation with their purchasing procedures. Too often, school districts frequently buy half a product when investing in computers. The infrastructure is installed without a compelling curriculum value supporting it. Consequently, teachers who have not yet embraced the new technologies and see no value to the hardware sprouting up on desks become technology-reluctant. Teachers expect a significant difference in outcomes and have little tolerance for change unless there is "compelling evidence" that the investment will have big dividends.

Imaging Computers as Resource and Learning Tool

To acclimate teachers in the school to the use of computers as both resource and learning tool, the author developed a nonthreatening, fun, learner-friendly environment that created skills that could quickly be integrated into the teaching process. (This project was subsequently included in the lead author's thesis, titled "No Teacher Left Behind.") A common denominator that was both alluring and motivational to most teachers was a love of travel. To build on this premise, a program brochure was designed that combined exotic Caribbean travel with an opportunity to experience the process of random learning that is an integral part of computer surfing. The goal for each teacher was to design a personal Caribbean vacation devoid of children and students. A practical and meaningful reward was provided: a travel agency donated gift certificates that could be used in purchasing the resulting getaway. To further galvanize the imagination of the participants, the training area was decorated with full-size vacation posters provided by the travel agency.

Each participant had hands-on experience using search engines, refining search phrase parameters, evaluating website descriptions for appropriateness, employing website page navigation skills, downloading and archiving relevant data, and evaluating the efficiency and user-friendliness of websites. As part of the process, the educators gained personal experience differentiating between random learning and structured learning. The evaluation of the program included observation by the media specialist and a feedback questionnaire.

There were several surprises regarding the expertise levels of the participants. With some, the level of expertise was much lower than had been anticipated. Two participants did not know how to turn on the computer, one expressed surprise that the data on the computer screen could be saved to other media, and one asked, "What's a flippy [sic]?" Those participants who were more knowledgeable teamed up with those who were not, an unintended but positive result.

The follow-up questionnaire revealed the high level of information the participants had acquired and the comfort zone they now had as a result of the collaboration in the workshop. As one participant enthused, "I learned more in this one workshop than I did in many others. We were all in the same boat and I didn't feel like I was the dummy in the class."

Teaching Information and Technology Skills

A restructuring of reference services will also become a part of the changing library program. The demands of technologies with traditional services will not work. It is a huge benefit to students when teachers work jointly with a professional who is trained to research, analyze, and retrieve information (i.e., the library media specialist). As the original information specialist, a school librarian must look at curricula, assignments, and learning in terms of the information resources, processes, and technologies required for student success. School librarians have been pioneers in teaching information skills and integrating technology skills into the information problem-solving process. One of the most popular approaches to integrated information and technology skills is the Big6 (Big6.com) approach, developed by Mike Eisenberg and Bob Berkowitz. The Big6 is a process model of how people of all ages solve an information problem. Eisenberg and Berkowitz found that successful information problem-solving encompasses six stages, with two substages under each, known as the Big6 Skills:

1. **Task Definition**
1.1 Define the information problem
1.2 Identify information needed

2. **Information Seeking Strategies**
2.1 Determine all possible sources
2.2 Select the best sources

3. **Location and Access**
3.1 Locate sources (intellectually and physically)
3.2 Find information within sources

4. **Use of Information**
4.1 Engage (e.g., read, hear, view, touch)
4.2 Extract relevant information

5. **Synthesis**
5.1 Organize from multiple sources
5.2 Present the information

6. **Evaluation**
6.1 Judge the product (effectiveness)
6.2 Judge the process (efficiency) ("What Is the Big6?" 2014)

School librarians need to do a better job of clearly articulating their roles in preparing students for the information-rich and technology-rich workplace of the future. It is essential for school librarians to commit themselves to the four central principles that define their roles as information specialists and educators helping students to achieve optimum use of information literacy:

> **Principle One:** The library is not a place; rather, the library is every-where. Beyond the school environment, students will need to make library skills part of their daily lives. Information problem-solving skills help students on a daily basis.
>
> **Principle Two:** Library and information professionals should be flexi-ble. Their roles include teacher, instructional partner, information spe-cialist, and program administrator.
>
> **Principle Three:** Ensure that students are effective users of ideas and information. All members of the school community need to under-stand that the library media specialist is uniquely qualified, valuable, and able to provide essential information literacy instruction and valu-able information services.
>
> **Principle Four:** Information is everywhere, essential, and central.

As to the effects the new role of the school librarian will have on the school library media center, implementing this new role will present a variety of challenges that will have to be solved in order for a school library media center to function effectively in an information-intensive society. The roles of the school librarian and the school library will continually change, and there-by create new challenges, as the images of information shift due to advancing technologies.

The Role of Reference for Today's School Librarian

So, with the elimination of print materials and their supplanting by digital me-dia, what is the role of the reference librarian? As Susan J. Beck (2015) stated in chapter 3 of this book, "the very core of reference services is the notion that librarians help users find the information they need. The librarian remains the intermediary between users and the information they seek" (27). Today, though, the school librarian is not thumbing through a stack of three-by-five cards in an oak drawer. Instead, the librarian's fingers dance across a keyboard, seeking the right combination of search words to assist the inquiring patron. And assistance is indisputably needed. Why? Let us explore the concept espoused by some that with all the information available at our fingertips on the World Wide Web, assistance, particularly that of a well-educated, paid individual (the reference librarian), is no longer required.

Upon receiving a research assignment from an instructor, today's typical student will turn to the World Wide Web for information. It is simply easier to key in a search word or phrase than to pick up a hefty reference tome in a library and attempt to navigate the index. In fact, in the not-too-distant future, those hefty reference volumes may become obsolete. Consider that on April 14, 2012, Encyclopedia Britannica, Inc. announced that it was discontinuing its print version and was going to sell only a digital version online—thus ends an era that began in1768 (Kearney 2012).

However, the way in which a search word or phrase is entered can have a tremendous effect on the search results. Unfortunately, today's students most often do not have any training in how to pare down a search phrase for the most relevant results, resulting in frustration or that old fallback—copy and paste—without any attempt at understanding.

Let us examine, hypothetically, what might happen if a middle or high school student is given a social studies assignment. For the sake of this discussion, let us assume the project is to determine the sociological impact of Native Americans teaching early Puritan settlers to grow corn. Typically, a web browser will default to Google or Bing as the search engine.

Using *corn* as a search word, Google provides 35,800,000 links. Bing provides 277,000,000 links. The student might then try to refine the search by using a phrase, *raising corn*, Google responds with 24,000,000 links, whereas Bing provides a measly 19,800,000. A more au courant student might refine the panoptic search by keying in a more specific phrase, *Indians raising corn*, hoping to reduce the exhaustive number of links. Google now responds with 26,900,000 links (including those on Indian corn and how to make popcorn), while Bing provides 9,310,000—certainly an improvement.

At this point, with the guidance of a computer-savvy librarian, the student might take the plunge with a pared-down search phrase, *Native Americans teaching Pilgrims to raise corn*. Surely, this will compress the research field tremendously. Google reduces the number of links by a whopping 96 percent, down to a mere 1,570,000. Bing, on the other hand, reduces the number by only 92 percent, with a resulting 23,500,000 links.

Part of training students to search the web for the correct answer is to instruct them to use the "specific question" as the query. This will, in most cases, result in the appropriate answer becoming available in the first few links. (The lead author's own media center's website and blog posts a monthly "Question of the Month." At the end of the year, a random drawing of correct replies results in the student receiving a $100 savings bond.) The basic assumption on the part of most researchers viewing the links is that the most relevant ones will appear on the first page or two.

In the Google results, the third link listed on the first page is the question *What did the Indian's [sic] teach the Pilgrim's [sic]*? Surely, this is the answer to the student's quest. (Hopefully, the misuse of the apostrophe is simply a typing mistake.) Clicking on the link brings the viewer to the WikiAnswers website. Herein, with all its errors, is the statement:

> The Indian's [*sic*] taught the Pilgrim's [*sic*] to grow corn and other crops. They taught them the way of the cuntiferous brown man. The most famous Indian of all, Squanto taught the Pilgrim's [*sic*] how to use toilet paper as well as how to make a proper peace pipe.

At this point, any student worth his salt will throw up his hands in despair (or double over in unrestrained laughter), shut down the computer, and seek the assistance of the reference librarian! (Frighteningly, this link appeared prominently in two other search engines.) A more inquiring student may attempt to learn the definition of "cuntiferous." A further exploration of the web might connect the student to the Urban Dictionary, which has a rather titillating definition—one that definitely should not appear in the final report.

Again, to cite Susan Beck (2015) in chapter 3 of this book, the reference librarian is no longer the information gatekeeper; rather, the reference librarian is an educator, as well as a handyman who is the master of creating PDFs, the webmaster who can update wikis, and the mechanic who can make a truculent printer spit out copies for a frustrated patron. If, as Beck suggests, school librarians need to turn their focus away from building a solid reference collection and toward a digital reference and virtual library, then there must be some understanding of what that constitutes.

Conclusion

Are virtual libraries the wave of the future? *Yes and no.* Virtual libraries are here, today, in schools, homes, and anywhere a modem can be connected. Virtual libraries are already an integral part of our professional and private lives and have been for quite some time. The professional who does not keep abreast of technological advances will drown in the informational tsunami.

Many Ivy League universities currently provide freshmen with laptops as an integral tool of the learning experience. The practice is migrating beyond the high schools down to the middle school level. In the Long Branch, New Jersey, middle school system, 950 students in grades six through eight in January 2012 were issued Samsung Galaxy tablets. Although the devices are connected to the Internet at all times, student access is limited to using seventy educational applications. During the first four months of usage, no tablets were lost by students, according to school superintendent Michael Salvatore, who also claims that students have become more engaged in learning. The district plans eventually to issue tablets to all students in grades three through twelve ("N.J. Middle School" 2012). In practice, instead of students traveling to the library or media center for research, the library or media center will magically appear on their laps wherever and whenever needed. Thus, the school library and media center joins the ranks of other resources with 24/7 availability.

However, the students must be taught the techniques of researching, analyzing, and retrieving pertinent information. This is particularly crucial in the primary and secondary educational systems, where learning and researching skills are acquired. This, then, is one of the new roles of the media specialist.

The school librarian needs to be integrated into the entire curriculum-design process and be viewed by administrators, educators, and students as a valuable resource person. The role of the school librarian will no longer be that of a hand pointing toward a stack of books but, rather, of a mentor guiding all library users toward the appropriate source of virtual information.

The trained school librarian is also critical in the physical design of a library media center, calling into play all the various needs of different types of learners and making the library center a true center for the dissemination of information. For example, in the elementary schools, areas need to be set aside for storytelling, events, guest speakers, and visual presentations. On the middle and high school levels, in addition to the usual resource areas, space needs to be allocated for individual and group projects, media presentations, and quiet study. The school librarian must also keep abreast of the latest websites and other virtual resources available online in order to guide users to the most up-to-date sites. Unfortunately, many librarians of long standing are poorly equipped to provide such a diverse role. Hence, the educational system and the students will suffer.

Furthermore, the most pressing problem for libraries is not enabling its users to connect to the Internet; it is instead the fact that eighty million books (virtually all the books and periodicals published from the middle of the nineteenth century to just a few years ago) are printed on paper with a high acid content that turns brown and brittle before deteriorating completely. For example, of the twelve million books in the New York Public Library, 20 to 25 percent are in various stages of disintegration (von Hoffman 1996). If it were possible to digitize all the books and other materials in all the world's libraries, this disintegration would not be a concern, but that is not going to happen, because the cost of digitizing would soar into the hundreds of billions of dollars. Decisions have to be made as to what will, or will *not*, be digitized. The rest may very well be lost.

Even rushing into digitization is risky because formats change and, even today, information that was digitized many years ago cannot be read by contemporary computers. Look at the panic that ensued prior to the year 2000, when companies realized that software that had been running for years in antiquated computer languages had to be modified and the software specialists who knew the languages had all retired.

For the immediate future, virtual libraries will coexist with traditional physical libraries. Some users will prefer to curl up with a printed volume in an overstuffed chair, while other users will prefer to curl up with a laptop in an overstuffed chair. School librarians should embrace the new technology with prudence while maintaining a traditional model. Simply put, both options should be equally viable and available.

Gazing into our digital crystal ball twenty-five years into the future, the devices that are state-of-the-art today will be ensconced in museums. We cannot even imagine what electronic devices will then be in commonplace usage by high school students. However, it is fairly safe to assume that the school library/media center will consist primarily of digital recapture devices and the old-fashioned hard-copy volume will be a thing of the past. Based on past history, the evolution, nay, the revolution in school libraries and media centers will continue on an ever-increasing pace, similar to a snowball rolling down a steep hill. And so it coexists with education.

REFERENCES

Antonucci, Nicole. 2012. "MAT-AB Students Visit Media Center to 'Book a Nook.'" *Independent*, April 12. http://ind.gmnews.com/news/2012-04-12/Front_Page/MATAB_students_visit_media_center_to_Book_a_Nook.html.

Beck, Susan J. 2015. "The Real Reference Revolution: The Digital Library User." In *Reinventing Reference: How Libraries Deliver Value in the Age of Google*, edited by Katie Elson Anderson and Vibiana Bowman Cvetkovic, 27–45. Chicago: American Library Association.

Clark, Tanna M. 1991. "Flexible Scheduling in the Elementary Library Center." *Arkansas Libraries* 48: 11–14.

Corbett, Nic. 2012. "Retiring N.J. State Librarian Stresses Libraries' Continued Relevance in Digital Age." *The Star-Ledger*, March 12. www.nj.com/news/index.ssf/2012/03/retiring_nj_state_librarian_st.html.

Franco, Alejandro. 2006. "The Challenges of Virtual Education." *E-Jist* 7 (113). www.ascilite.org.au/ajet/e-jist/docs/Vol7_No1/MeltingPot/Challenges_virtual.htm.

Heyboer, Kelley. 2005. "College of New Jersey's $35M Gem Even Has a Starbucks in the Lobby." *The Star-Ledger*, October 18.

Hill, Michael. 2005. "Libraries Check Out Virtual World: Patrons Can Now Download Audiobooks." *The Star-Ledger*, August 26.

Kearney, Christine. 2012. "Encyclopedia Britannica Ends Print, Goes Digital." *Reuters*, March 14. www.reuters.com/assets/print?aid=USBRE82C1FS201220314.

Levin, Doug. 2011. "Closing Conversation: The Financing." New York Times Schools for Tomorrow: Bringing Technology into the Classroom conference, September 22, New York City.

Marsh, Merle. 2008. "Teachers Teaching Teachers." ComputerLearning.org. http://web.archive.org/web/20080516075841/http:/computerlearning.org/articles/TTT.htm.

Mehlinger, Howard D. 1996. "School Reform in the Information Age." *Phi Delta Kappan* 77 (6): 400–407.

"N.J. Middle School Ditches Textbooks for Tablets." 2012. *The Star-Ledger*, May 4. www.nj.com/news/index.ssf/2012/05/nj_middle_school_ditches_textb.html.

Oglesby, Amanda. 2012. "Teachers Tweet and Students Skype as Classrooms Go Digital." *The Asbury Park Press*, March 30.

Pentlin, Floyd. 2010. "Who're You Gonna Call? The "School Librarian." *AASL Blog*, January 17. www.aasl.ala.org/aaslblog/?p=913.

Prensky, Marc. 2001. "Digital Natives, Digital Immigrants." *On the Horizon* 9 (5): 1–2.

Richtel, Matt. 2011. "A Silicon Valley School That Doesn't Compute." *The New York Times*, October 22. www.nytimes.com/2011/10/23/technology/at-waldorf-school-in-silicon-valley-technology-can-wait.html?pagewanted=all&_r=0.

Schmidt, Janine, and Hamilton Wilson. 1998. "Designing the Real Virtual Library: An Overview of the Preparation of an Upgrade for the University of Queensland Library." In *Robots to Knowbots: The Wider Automation Agenda*, 5–6. Proceedings of the Victorian Association for Library Automation Conference, January 28–30, Melbourne, Australia. http://trove.nla.gov.au/version/166896575.

Schmidt, T., J. J. Croud, and D. Turnbull. 2000. "The University of Queensland Cybrary: A Virtual Library." In *World Libraries on the Information Superhighway: Preparing for the Challenges of the New Millennium*, edited by P. D. Fletcher and J. C. Bertot, 107–24. London: Idea Group.

Schuetze, Christopher F. 2011. "A Scholarly Role for Consumer Technology." *The New York Times*, November 23. www.nytimes.com/2011/11/24/world/europe/a-scholarly-role-for-consumer-technology.html?pagewanted=all.

Schwarz, Alan. 2012. "Mooresville's Shining Example (It's Not Just about the Laptops)." *The New York Times*, February 12. www.nytimes.com/2012/02/13/education/mooresville-school-district-a-laptop-success-story.html?pagewanted=all.

Squires, Tasha. 2009. *Library Partnerships: Making Connections between School and Public Libraries*. Medford, NJ: Information Today.

Staino, Rocco. 2010. "AASL Adopts 'School Librarian' As Official Term for Profession." *School Library Journal*, January 21 (archived article; no longer available to the public).

Summers, L. H. 2011. "Keynote Address." New York Times Schools for Tomorrow: Bringing Technology into the Classroom conference, September 22, New York City.

von Hoffman, Nicholas. 1996. "Checking Out Electronic Libraries: Repackaging Information for the Next Millennium." *Architectural Digest* 53 (10): 130–2.

"What Is the Big6?" 2014. Big6.com. Accessed August 25. http://big6.com/pages/about.php.

The Future of Public Library Reference

Justin Hoenke

The days of the reference desk being the heart of the public library are gone. "There used to be a phalanx of librarians at the reference desk at my public library," said librarian Lia Horton during a personal interview on September 16, 2011. "Their desk was front and center and you went there for any questions you had. That's gone now. Things have changed." What remains is a skeletal group of reference librarians, standing on the front line maintaining the peace. What happened to the patrons who used to storm the reference desk to find what they were looking for? They are most likely on their laptops finding exactly what they need in a matter of seconds.

Technology has drastically changed how reference librarians work. As James Keehbler, Director of the Piscataway (New Jersey) Public Library noted, "There are less reference questions, period. Nobody can convince me otherwise" (personal communication via Google Chat, September 16, 2011). As patrons become more comfortable with technology, the role of the librarian will change even more. This chapter investigates the impact of technology and the changing landscape of public library reference to see how the reference librarian fits into the picture of the twenty-first-century library.

The Presumed Death of Reference

At the time of this writing, the idea that "reference is dead" has been floating around. Eli Neiburger, the associate director for IT (information technology) and production at the Ann Arbor (Michigan) District Library, advocated that in order to advance the mission of the library, reference staff would need to be cut to pave the way to employ "geeks" in the library to look after the technology (Kelley 2011).

Neiburger continued: "Despite the fact that a trained librarian can bring value to a reference interaction, the patron today, acclimated to Google searches, does not feel that way, and librarians cannot change their mind" (Kelley 2011). As more and more information is disseminated on the Internet, access to this information is at more and more people's fingertips. On his blog, *Swiss Army Librarian*, Brian Herzog (2010) wrote that "for kids growing up with the Internet of today, this is their Web 1.0—because they've never known anything else."

But is reference dead? While exchange of information from the librarian to the patron may no longer be the model, the reference librarian is still alive and kicking. Still, the reference librarian as the information gatekeeper is a role that is no longer sustainable. To move ahead, reference librarians do not need to drastically cut ties to the past. Instead, they should embrace the past while at the same time changing to better accommodate the future of the profession. Reference librarians, once the gatekeepers of information, can now take that information to the next level with their patrons and educate them. Neiburger used the analogy of a travel agent: "Travel agents were outmoded because people felt they had better access to the information than they could get from the travel agents. We're in a similar sort of spot" (Kelley 2011).

New Roles for Today's Reference Librarian

The Librarian as Translator of Information

A role that librarians can embrace is that of a translator of information. It is a role that the reference librarian has perfected over the years through a never-ending series of interactions with patrons, yet the influence of technology has caused a shift in the expectations of patrons. Marion Peterson, a reference librarian at the Walker Memorial Library in Westbrook, Maine, is a perfect example of this new role in action. In a personal communication via e-mail on September 16, 2011, Peterson stated, "I'm not certain I do 'reference' these days; I am social worker, hand-holder, cheerleader, computer techie (limited!), and listener. Each library/librarian and the services we offer are directly related to our community and to our patrons." The reference librarian today is the modern-day hydra, with each head acting a different role for the patrons using the library.

Peterson's description of her day-to-day work is a snapshot of what most public librarians who are working in any kind of reference are doing. So much of the role that the reference librarian plays has become less about offering a specific service to patrons. Instead, what the reference librarian does is offer a service that really cannot be described in one word or singular concept. It is sort of this job that is out there, floating in the ether. Reference librarians provide a service, but this service is not specific and is difficult to define. One minute it can be helping someone find a particular book, and the next minute it could entail editing a résumé. This kind of job has its major benefits (how could someone ever get bored?), yet at the same time it has given librarians a bit of an identity crisis. What does a reference librarian actually do? This chapter argues that the role of librarian is akin to that of a music producer. A music producer's role is to help the artist translate what is in his or her head into something tangible and listenable. The producer (the librarian) listens to the artist (the patron) and his or her needs and then translates those demands into something that the engineer (aka databases, books, media) can understand. The end product is something that predominantly shows the work of the patron, but the expertise of the librarian is seen as well.

However, questions remain. How can the reference librarian adapt to this change when there is so much to do? Is it not best to be really good at one thing instead of average at all of these other little things? This idea is no longer sustainable if public library reference wishes to remain relevant in the twenty-first century. Reference librarians need to adapt and embrace the roles of educator and collaborator.

The Librarian as Trainer

One model that could shape the future of public library reference is the concept of the librarian as educator/trainer. The goals of the modern-day librarian working reference should be in line with that of an educator. Looking closely at school librarians points toward ideas of what should be done in regard to training communities. In the article "Pivot Points for Change," Buffy Hamilton (2010) highlighted two key points to engage patrons: maintain traditional means of connecting, sharing, and productivity, but embrace innovation and encourage collaboration and sharing. These key points offer the reference librarian of the twenty-first century an outline as the public library changes. The following two sections in this chapter explore these concepts more completely.

Librarians are a community resource. Modern librarians must balance their undying love for the library profession with an approach that is more social. Being right there on the front line of the battle with the patrons is the first step. Today's reference librarian must become part of the overall fabric of the community.

If patrons are not coming into the library to seek something specific anymore, why are they still coming? Sure, most of them want a specific item that the library holds, but there has to be something more than that. That patrons will adopt certain librarians as their favorite librarians, whom they consult no matter what kind of support they need, shows that being a librarian is about the bigger picture of acting as a community resource first and a librarian second. The Falmouth (Massachusetts) Public Library followed this trend by holding an event called "The Library as a Community Resource." This event focused on partnerships the library had formed with groups and individual people in Falmouth to better serve the community (Bordonaro 2011).

Technological support is another tool in the librarian utility belt that must be mastered. A lot of today's reference work centers around the questions "How can I do this?," "How can I share this?," and "How can I create this?" Reference librarians today must take it upon themselves to explore technology and provide patrons with a quality experience.

Michael Stephens and Aaron Schmidt take the stance that user experience (UX) is a key element on which public libraries need to focus to effectively engage patrons. The key takeaway from the writings of Stephens and Schmidt (2011) is that "[g]ood information architecture combats information overload." This suggests that the librarian who thinks of the patron and his or her needs first will be one step ahead, having already provided tech support through good UX.

Finally, one of the best ways for librarians to adapt to the added role of a trainer is to immerse themselves in a setting where they will be faced with unique experiences. Librarians who are fresh out of graduate school may find it beneficial to spend a good bit of time on the public reference desk. Working "in the trenches" gives a librarian real-life experience.

The day-to-day interactions librarians have with patrons are shaping the library of the future. Every library has patrons who come in every day and have their specific routines. These are the patrons who are using library services the most. These are the patrons to whom libraries should be reaching out. Opening up communication with our patrons is the first step. It starts with a hello, and in time, this simple introduction could lead to the patron becoming a more active user of the library, one who is more engaged in and values the reference services offered.

Collaboration and Information Sharing

Cloud computing can be defined as an "updated version of utility computing: basically virtual servers available over the Internet" (Knorr and Gruman 2011). What this breaks down to is simple: cloud computing allows users to access information and tools that are stored off-site. Many times, these tools are collaborative in nature. The idea of having a program or a file stored somewhere other than on a device that only one person can access (e.g., USB drive, hard drive, disc) opens it up to be something that encourages collaboration.

Many handy and free tools out there embrace cloud computing. One example of a cloud computing tool used by many public library patrons today is Google Docs, which is a free, web-based collection of productivity tools including a word processor, spreadsheets, and more. Patrons who have a Google account have access to Google Docs and can access all of these tools for their personal use. Access to this type of resource allows libraries greater flexibility in collaborating with patrons. Patrons can share documents and questions with librarians with great ease, with no worries about file formats or any kind of system compatibility. Another online tool that uses cloud computing to encourage sharing and collaboration is Evernote, basically an online notebook that stores writings, images, and more. An individual can use Evernote to collect ideas, notes, research, and more and then share these with the reference librarian to facilitate collaboration. Finally, a newer online tool that librarians have been looking into for possible uses to engage patrons is Pinterest, which acts as an online pinboard for things the user finds on the Internet. The Library as Incubator Project (2012) uses Pinterest to develop pinboards with specific themes on how libraries can work with artists and art organizations to develop creative programs that engage patrons.

Easy access to collaboration gives librarians more time to focus on what patrons need. This is key to the twenty-first-century reference librarians' success in clearly communicating their worth to the community.

Balancing the Traditional and the Trendy

In regard to serving younger generations, library reference is a whole different ball game. One notable change that the reference librarian will see in providing younger patrons with reference is that, as the years pass, interest in obtaining the information through the physical printed medium has waned. To keep current with this trend, librarians who serve children and teens have turned their focus away from building a solid print reference collection and toward digital reference and finding quality tools and information that can be accessed online for free. In the 2011 Periodicals Price Survey at *Library Journal*, EBSCO reported that "more than 80 percent of librarian respondents indicated that they were likely to move print plus online subscriptions to online only in order to achieve budget goals" (Bosch, Henderson, and Klusendorf 2011). Looking at it from a broad perspective, this is still part of the mission of providing access to quality information and tools to the community. Providing younger patrons with access to resources they can use as they multitask online has become a tool librarians can use to engage patrons more fully.

One of the greater obstacles that reference librarians face when working with students is the belief that the "container" actually affects the quality of information. Librarians know that what an online database or a well-produced online document gives patrons is no less in terms of quality than information found in a printed reference source. However, looking at this from a different perspective shows that this is not the case with patrons. Teen library patrons who come into the library for assistance with a simple research paper often remark that one of the rules for their work is that they cannot use the Internet. This is a blow to librarians, as it immediately rules out using a credible online database purchased by the library exactly for this reason.

Rebecca Hill (2010), in her article on multitasking teens, pointed out some staggering statistics that show just how dramatically the container in which information is delivered is changing: "Cell phone ownership has increased from 39 percent in 2004 to 66 percent in 2010. Seventy six percent own iPods. According to U.S. Census data, 76.6 percent of all three to seventeen year olds live in a household with Internet access" (33). These statistics clearly point toward the shift that is happening in regard to how the younger generation is accessing information. In finding, developing, and sharing these tools with younger patrons, the reference librarian will be assisting in creating a community that is information literate. Hill also explained that information literacy means that libraries have the unique opportunity to take the lead in teaching teens how to use . . . technologies appropriately through programming" (35). The only way that public reference librarians can effectively create a more informed citizenry of patrons is to meet them where they are gathered, and a big part of that rests in librarians being able to understand, use, and disseminate information through the containers that patrons are using.

The final step that public librarians need to take is one that involves a bit of advocacy. Public librarians need to better communicate their worth and expand services to illustrate how they benefit public education. Whether this involves providing patrons with classes on effective research and database use or performing outreach to local teachers to show them the tools libraries offer to students, libraries must undertake these efforts to survive and weave themselves into the community. Libraries need to be staffed with librarian-educators who have the opportunity to teach community members the digital skills they need. Susie Andretta (2009) from the London Metropolitan University stated that "libraries are already meeting the challenges of transliteracy by crossing the divide between printed, digital and virtual worlds to address the constantly changing needs of the learners they support" (2). The interactions that librarians have with their patrons will help bridge the digital divide and improve transliteracy.

The easiest thing to learn and, at the same time, the easiest thing to forget about reference work is that it is all about people. Aaron Schmidt (2011) wrote, "Quality reference work takes more than just being able to construct a complicated Boolean search; it takes social intelligence, too." Librarians often overlook this simple ingredient when connecting with other people. Reference librarians should be kind to one another and to patrons when working at the reference desk. This is a key ingredient in reference librarianship, especially given that the role of the reference librarian is to work with the community. Reference librarianship involves interaction with other people. Being kind to one another allows the reference interactions to flourish and gives patrons the quality service they were looking for when they came to the library.

Reference librarians must embrace the idea that expanded services are needed to reflect patron needs. Librarians need to embrace the educator role. One-on-one reference interactions are great, but librarians should consider the possibilities of educating communities through library programs.

The interactions the community has with the librarians do not have to be about tools that the library purchases or training patrons. Librarians have always been known as information seekers. Reference librarians and their passion to explore and learn has helped this far, and it is something that should not be forgotten as reference librarianship evolves. Searching out new ways of approaching librarianship is something that should be actively pursued by everyone in the profession. This idea, which is akin to playing in the sandbox, allows part of the reference librarian's job to be all about exploring.

A good example of seeking out new ways of approaching librarianship is through use of tools such as Historypin (www.historypin.com), an online, user-generated archive of historical photos and personal recollections. Patrons using this service can use the location and date of an image to "pin" it to Google Maps. When collected, these photos offer anyone viewing a Historypin map a detailed, historical look at their surroundings. Librarians not only can use this service themselves to add photos and information to their local communities' Historypin maps but also can encourage their patrons to do the same. This is a great way to build a local collection and move the information into the twenty-first century. Libraries that can mobilize some volunteers to digitize photos and upload them to Historypin can enrich their collection. Libraries could even partner with local tourism organizations to give people with mobile phones a walking history tour of the city or develop library programming aimed at local historians who use their talents and Historypin to grow the local collections.

The Library Patron of the Future

Today's teenagers will become our adult users soon, and with that, a radical shift in how the library is used will happen. Simply stated, teens are not using the library the way that librarians envision most people are using the library. In her article "What's Right with This Picture? Chicago's YOUmedia Reinvents the Public Library," Karen Springen (2011) provided an in-depth examination of what public library reference may look like very soon. Instead of relying on librarians as their information seekers, library patrons are on the hunt for information themselves.

YOUmedia, a space in the Chicago Public Library that is aimed at providing services to teens, is described as a "free digital media workshop where paid teen mentors share the latest scoop on everything from graphic design and digital photography to designing digital games and creating fan fiction and films" (Springen 2011). The guiding principle behind the YOUmedia center is best summarized by Springen (2011): "Creative learning—using digital media and other technology—is the key." The tools traditionally offered by libraries, combined with resources like the ones mentioned earlier in this chapter, all sewn together with the social intelligence that the public reference librarian uses with patrons will help guide the library patrons of the future.

It is clear that a monumental shift has occurred with the way patrons use libraries. Patrons in the past came to the library to seek a specific thing, whereas the teen library users of today, the adult library users of the future, are seeking experiences. Justin Busque, a teen patron at the Portland (Maine) Public Library, put it this way: "I come here to hang out, to talk with people I enjoy being around, and to just enjoy life." With this knowledge, reference librarians can see teen populations using the library as the litmus test for how libraries can radically restructure their ideas and approaches toward reference.

The Changing Landscape of Print Reference

So far, this chapter has focused mainly on providing reference in a digital age, but what about print reference? With all due respect to the wonderful printed book, print reference in the public library is going the way of the dodo. As people turn more and more to computers for information, reference books are left on the shelves to collect dust.

In 2008, Sue Polanka noted that print reference was on its way out, and her insights are still spot on today:

> Why isn't our print reference collection getting used? Partly because it's invisible! There are several factors that explain the invisibility predicament. First, the Y factor. For Generation Y, born with a laptop, cell phone, and iPod in their hands, print reference books are not part of the research process and probably never will be.

Buried behind rows of shelves, these hulking masses of reference books were sitting there in 2008, waiting for someone to use them. And they are still sitting there, waiting for someone to use them.

This is not to say that print reference collections should all be recycled at this very moment. At this time, which is one of serious transition for public libraries, print reference still holds a great deal of worth for patrons. While topics like digital reference and real-time collaboration are very much a reality, they are still quite new to the patrons who are using our libraries. For many patrons, their way of viewing the library is steeped in the belief that the library is the collector of the printed word. Librarians need to make sure that the public library is as cutting-edge as possible, but not so much so that a segment of users is left behind.

There is great cost associated with investing in print reference. These hulking sets of books are not just a drop in the financial bucket, but a long-term investment. Libraries that still invest portions of their budgets into print reference have to look closely at a few factors. First, and perhaps the most important thing to consider, is whether the information in these books will be out of date by the time they are cataloged and shelved. In a quickly changing world, how can the printed reference book stay relevant? The answer is that it cannot. When choosing print reference resources, librarians must select titles with information that will likely remain relevant for some years to come, thus validating the investment in these materials. The next questions to be asked rely on the investigation skills of the librarian: Is there other information out there that can be easily accessed and delivered to patrons in a way that they can use it? Can the librarian find the materials patrons need online and prepare some kind of print package in lieu of purchased reference materials? This idea echoes the words of Keehbler at the start of this chapter: with fewer reference questions, librarians should be taking the extra time to provide more in-depth and more personalized service. This goes against the thinking presented by Neiburger (Kelley 2011), as it would most certainly call for an increased need in public library reference staff. However, it does present a possible way forward, one whereby print reference can be slowly phased out in favor of digital reference. The service that then takes the place of print reference is one based solely on human interaction, with the librarians as the experts and guides and the patrons as the learners. This offers public library reference a brighter future, one guided by the always strong belief that no matter how much the world changes, librarians will always still have one another for help.

What is clear is that a two-part solution is needed if libraries are to continue to invest a significant portion of budgets toward reference. Libraries need to be investing in quality digital reference and, at the same time, training staff to teach the community how to access this wealth of knowledge. Librarians are the generals whose job is to train patrons and communities to become an army of information seekers.

Approaches to Digital Reference Delivery

The question of how to deliver content to patrons is something reference librarians should be looking at very closely. Providing patrons with e-mail links to articles will work sometimes, but there has to be more to the transactions than that. Librarians today must understand their options for delivering material. They must become masters of creating PDFs, updating wikis, and, yes, still something as simple as making copies for patrons. They must adapt to the needs of the patrons first. A good example of this can be seen in the digital reference setup that the Topeka and Shawnee County (Kansas) Public Library (http://tscpl.org) has adopted. Although they are still referring to the databases by the product names, librarians have grouped the databases by subject and provided each database with a simple explanation that patrons can read to help them understand what they are using.

The solution of turning completely toward digital reference is not without its flaws. Digital reference collections may be hidden from the public view, and if users cannot find them, are they really there? Polanka (2008) shared insight into this idea:

> I've already discussed how ineffective the catalog is in retrieving content inside our titles. Unfortunately, this leaves the user with searching the vendor interfaces—all of them, individually. This is cumbersome and ineffective. It's time for publishers to start playing together in the same "searchbox."

Here is where librarians need to become more active with the vendors from whom they are purchasing databases. The interfaces seen and used for digital reference sources vary wildly. A librarian might become a master of one of these databases only to have to turn around and learn a whole new system for another database. This certainly is hard on librarians, but imagine how difficult it is for patrons. In a world where Google returns instant search results, who wants to spend time learning the eccentricities of a database?

So what can librarians do? They can demand better products and customization from vendors. Databases that allow librarians and patrons to customize the experience will provide for a greater overall experience for all involved. A good example of taking initiative and working directly with vendors comes from the recent discussions between the leaders of the American Library Association and publishers regarding e-books and library lending (Kelley 2012).

The other alternative libraries can look toward is a hybrid model, one that combines both cumbersome database searches and instant Google results. After all, is not balance a good thing? Libraries must embrace the instant results of Google and teach patrons how to use them effectively. This kind of education in using Google can also lead patrons to understand what constitutes an effective database search. A Google search is actually a good example of what not to do when using a database. It can also be a good example of how to locate materials that may not be otherwise available through databases. Blogs and social media are great examples of just how important a Google search can be for a patron. Over the past few years, the use of blogging and social media as news sources has been on the rise. It has graduated from being viewed solely as a hobby or a means of personal communication into a serious form of journalism. In her discussion of the Crystal Cox (a blogger who was sued for defamation) case, Ellyn Angelotti (2011) of the Poynter Institute argued in her *New York Times* piece, "Blogs compete with mainstream media every day. In some cases, they have become more trustworthy as sources of information than some old school practitioners." News agencies such as the New York Times Company, CNN, and others have all turned to blogging to share breaking news and opinion pieces. Tools such as Google Blog Search (www .google.com/blogsearch) can go a long way for patrons. Effective use of social media sites, such as Twitter, Facebook, and more, can also lead patrons to better search results. Libraries are already holding classes, for example, the "Facebook for Seniors" class offered by the Portland Public Library (2012). Showing patrons these tools and teaching them about the culture and style of blogging and social media will open their eyes to a new form of information.

There is also the tricky subject of e-books. While, at the time of this writing, everything having to do with e-books seems a bit up in the air, a clearer path is slowly coming to the surface, as evidenced by the meeting between the American Library Association and book publishers (Kelley 2012). As with Google Docs and other collaborative tools in the previous sections, e-books allow the librarian to easily share ideas and information with patrons. One interesting example is the ability to share notes and passages through the Amazon Kindle with others via Facebook and Twitter. Patrons who actively use these networks can then interact with their librarians over them and share information through e-books.

Conclusion

The future of reference in the public library will be heavily influenced by the connection between the patron and the librarian, much like the examples mentioned earlier in this chapter. This personalized service allows the librarian to be better in tune with the needs of the specific patron. In an uncertain future, where only certain book publishers allow their e-books to be circulated in libraries and where access to the Internet allows the patron to easily find information without assistance, developing a connection with patrons allows libraries to have a unique advantage: the personalized touch.

In "Using Social Media to Connect with Teens," the author (Hoenke 2010) discussed how using social media profiles to interact with patrons opened up a new level in providing reference to patrons:

> When one teen found that [he] and I shared an interest in [the band] The Mars Volta, he came running in the library one day in disbelief. He was excited that I was into the same music as him. He now comes in a few times each week and we spend a good fifteen minutes or so talking about music. This is just one of countless examples of how opening up my personal social networking accounts to teens has made it easier for me to connect with them and provide them with quality service. In the end, it makes you more of a real person to them. They become your friend and they trust you. The upside to this? They're using the library . . . and they love it.

To reinvent reference in the public library, the librarians of the future will take center stage and use their position to help empower a community toward greatness.

REFERENCES

Andretta, Susie. 2009. "Transliteracy: Take a Walk on the Wild Side." Presented at World Library and Information Congress: 75th IFLA General Conference and Council, August 27–29. http://eprints.rclis.org/14868/1/94-andretta-en.pdf.

Angelotti, Ellyn. 2011. "We Need a Broader Definition of 'Journalist.'" *The New York Times*, December 11. www.nytimes.com/roomfordebate/2011/12/11/are-all-bloggers-journalists/we-need-a-broader-definition-of-journalist.

Bordonaro, Fran. 2011. "Library as a Community Resource." *Falmouth Public Library of Massachusetts* (blog), April 16. www.falmouthpubliclibrary.org/?/blog/entries/library-as-a-community-resource.

Bosch, Stephen, Kittie Henderson, and Heather Klusendorf. 2011. "Periodicals Price Survey 2011: Under Pressure, Times Are Changing." *Library Journal*, April 14. http://lj.libraryjournal.com/2011/04/publishing/periodicals-price-survey-2011-under-pressure-times-are-changing/.

Hamilton, Buffy. 2010. "Pivot Points for Change with Buffy Hamilton—Archived Session." Georgia Public Library Service Webinar, June 16. http://buffyjhamilton.wordpress.com/tag/pivot-points-for-change.

Herzog, Brian. 2010. "Digital Natives Are Not—They Just Are." *Swiss Army Librarian* (blog), March 4. www.swissarmylibrarian.net/2010/03/04/digital-natives-are-not-they-just-are/.

Hill, Rebecca. 2010. "The World of Multitasking Teens: How Library Programming Is Changing to Meet These Needs." *Young Adult Library Services* 8 (4): 33–36.

Hoenke, Justin. 2010. "Using Social Media to Connect with Teens." *Tame the Web* (blog), March 17. http://tametheweb.com/2010/03/17/using-social-media-to-connect-with-teens.

Kelley, Michael. 2011. "Geeks Are the Future: A Program in Ann Arbor, MI, Argues for a Resource Shift Toward IT." *Library Journal*, April 26. http://lj.libraryjournal.com/2011/04/technology/geeks-are-the-future-a-program-in-ann-arbor-mi-argues-for-a-resource-shift-toward-it.

———. 2012. "ALA Leaders Also to Meet with Executives from Random House." *Library Journal*, January 26. www.thedigitalshift.com/2012/01/ebooks/ala-leaders-also-to-meet-with-executives-from-random-house.

Knorr, Eric, and Galen Gruman. 2011. "What Cloud Computing Really Means." InfoWorld: Cloud Computing. Accessed September 3. www.infoworld.com/d/cloud-computing/what-cloud-computing-really-means-031.

Library as Incubator Project. 2012. "IArtLibraries Is Now on Pinterest!" *The Library as Incubator Project* (blog), January 17. www.libraryasincubatorproject.org/?p=2516.

Polanka, Sue. 2008. "Off the Shelf: Is Print Reference Dead?" *Booklist Online*, January 1. www.booklistonline.com/ProductInfo.aspx?pid=2403576&AspxAutoDetect CookieSupport=1.

Portland Public Library. 2012. "Facebook for Seniors." Accessed February 29. www.portlandlibrary.com/programs/FacebookforSeniorsFeb.2012.pdf (no longer available); see instead www.portlandlibrary.com/programs.

Schmidt, Aaron. 2011."Revamping Reference." *Walking Paper: A Library Design Consultancy, Shop and Blog*, October 17. www.walkingpaper.org/4184.

Springen, Karen. 2011. "What's Right with This Picture? Chicago's YOUmedia Reinvents the Public Library." *School Library Journal: Library News, Reviews and Views*, March 1. www.slj.com/2011/03/technology/whats-right-with-this-picture -chicagos-youmedia-reinvents-the-public-library/#_.

Stephens, Michael, and Aaron Schmidt. 2011. "Putting the UX in Education: The User Experience + Office Hours." *Library Journal*, July 15. http://lj.libraryjournal.com/ 2011/07/library-education/putting-the-ux-in-education-the-user-experience -office-hours.

The Central Image
The Future of Reference in Academic Arts Libraries

Sara Harrington

The focus of this chapter is an examination of the future of reference in a particular type of library—the academic arts library. In the triumvirate of library types—academic, public, and special—arts libraries can be found in each category. As such, it seems apt to use the arts library as a case study for the future of reference in special libraries. In addition, while the concept of "the image" is the organizing principle and driving force behind the work of art librarians, visual culture itself has become increasingly important to interdisciplinary scholarship. Issues regarding image-based collections and institutional digitization initiatives are of importance to a wide range of information professionals. This chapter is intended to encourage library professionals to consider how extant image-related services and collections can be used to reach new audiences, to reevaluate the "special collections" the library holds and who the audiences for such collections might be, and to reexamine the library's relationship to the image.

As in all libraries, the future landscape of arts librarianship will be defined by resource constriction, a digitization imperative, and an assessment mandate. This chapter examines these issues in turn in regard to libraries in general, and then in the context of reference services in academic arts libraries in particular. The discussion begins by defining reference and reviewing the state of reference services in academic libraries. Next, selected top trends identified by the Association of College and Research Libraries (ACRL) are used as a lens through which to view the challenges facing arts libraries. Finally, a consideration of the future of reference in academic arts libraries concludes with thoughts about assessment, an important consideration as arts information professionals strive to demonstrate the value of arts libraries—and their collections and services—to the institutions, all while honoring their own values as professionals in service to students and other patrons. Given the proliferation of online images, arts information professionals no longer serve as gatekeepers to the image. Instead, arts information professionals can bring their critical intelligence, experience, and skill sets to educating students and others about the image and its use.

Defining Reference in Academic Arts Libraries

The focus in this discussion is on arts libraries in which arts information professionals provide reference services drawing on so-called "traditional" collections of books, journals, and electronic resources, as well as those arts libraries which, in addition to traditional collections, may include rarely held primary sources and/or unique collections of objects and artifacts. Arts information professionals also provide reference services based on information found freely available on the web, mine resources available at institutions other than their own, and network with colleagues in the field in order to respond to queries and advance research and scholarship. The term "arts information professional" is used in recognition of the fact that reference services in academic arts libraries are performed by librarians and by skilled paraprofessionals and, sometimes, by trained student workers. This discussion uses an expansive definition of reference in arts libraries since changes in reference are increasingly seen as a part of wider discussions of transformations in liaison relationships and services to broad-based user communities. The references referred to in this chapter highlight the wealth of resources that exist on both reference and arts librarianship in the twenty-first century (Radford and Lankes 2010; Wilson 2003).

One of the more recent "hot" topics—the potential elimination of the reference desk—is not examined. Although the subject of current debate in recent literature and in the field (Arndt 2010), the end of the reference desk is in some ways symbolic of fears about the perceived obsolescence of librarianship. Decisions about radically altering or eliminating the physical reference desk are based on local conditions, historical relationships of the campus with the library, financial and personnel resources, and other factors. Eliminating the reference desk does not eradicate reference. Instead, the definitions of reference within the field must become much broader as librarians continue to move from reactive to proactive models of reference services. Rather than offering specific recommendations, this chapter explores larger issues surrounding the future of reference in academic arts libraries, and in the work of arts information professionals, and demonstrates the value and potential of both.

The State of Reference Services

In recent years, arts information professionals, like the staff of other libraries, have engaged in wide-ranging experimentation in providing reference services. These experiments generally fall into a few broad categories: staffing the reference desk, reaching beyond the physical reference desk, and using a range of technologies to provide reference services. Kay Ann Cassel (2010) usefully and succinctly summarized these trends in "Meeting Users' Needs through New Reference Service Models." Cassel stated that libraries have employed tiered reference services, which use trained paraprofessional staff, to answer directional and other frontline reference questions, while referring more in-depth queries to reference librarians. Library administrators have also encouraged their staff to engage in roving reference, during which librarians circulate through the reference room and other parts of the library to make themselves more visible and approachable and to proactively connect with patrons who may appear to need assistance (Cassel 2010).

Cassel (2010) noted that another current trend is mobile librarianship, that is, librarians leaving the library building altogether and working from other campus outposts or embedding within departments where potential users may be concentrated. As Carlson and Kneale (2011) explained: "Embedded librarianship takes a librarian out of the context of the traditional library and places him or her in an 'on-site' setting or situation that enables close coordination and collaboration with researchers or teaching faculty" (167). Carlson and Kneale drew a helpful distinction between two different types of embedding: that which is permanent or programmatic in nature versus that which is temporary or project based, intended to advance a specific project, jump-start a particular initiative, or provide enhanced service to users at a particular moment in time.

Embedding has arguably provided some of the more promising opportunities for reviving reference and extending the possibilities for collaborations between librarians and their primary users (Kvenild and Calkins 2011). The embedded librarian becomes part of the life and work flow of the program or department in which he or she works, in ways that might not be possible with more episodic contact. The emphasis in embedded librarianship is on meeting users in reference exchanges where *they* are—as opposed to asking users to come to the librarian. Embedded librarianship has taken place across libraries against the background of an overall and trending decline in reference transactions (Novotny 2002). While in some libraries there has been a decline in traditional transactions at the reference desk, at others there has been an increase or, at minimum, a shift in workload (Applegate 2008). As reference is conducted via multiple modes, questions may be transferred from one format to another (e.g., from live chat to e-mail), referred to a subject or other specialist, or followed up on as necessary to fully respond to a query. Much embedded librarianship is accomplished through the librarian's presence in courses in course management systems, which serve a wide range of traditional, hybrid, and distance learning students. Perhaps in part because of a decline in in-person reference, librarians have placed a renewed focus on close engagement with users via embedded librarianship and other models.

In conducting these experiments, reference librarians have also progressively adopted advancing technology to provide reference. In addition to in-person and telephone reference, librarians routinely use e-mail, live chat, and text messaging to answer reference questions, and they continue to experiment with social software (Cassel 2010). At the conclusion of periods of reference experimentation and trials, final choices about where and how reference services will be offered, who will staff reference services, the hours reference services will be provided, and the technologies used to provide reference are often based on the resources available (most commonly in the form of personnel). Other important considerations are the architectural and space planning concerns related to the reference desk, the reference room, and the library building itself. Yet another factor is the geographic location of the library building on campus, and its proximity to potential users. It is likely that there will be continued experimentation with reference and an increasing movement to virtual reference in lieu of in-person reference. One challenge will continue to be listening to and responding to users' ongoing feedback about academic reference services in an agile and flexible manner, without overreacting or making far-reaching changes too quickly or without a critical mass of feedback.

Challenges to Reference Services in Arts Libraries

One way to begin thinking about the future of reference in arts libraries is by considering the current trends in libraries more generally, while focusing on those issues that seem most likely to affect the work of arts libraries for some time to come. The ACRL Planning and Review Committee's "2010 Top Ten Trends in Academic Libraries" pointed to a range of issues affecting all libraries. The focus here is on a few specific trends taken from ACRL's forecast. Arts libraries in particular may be arguably most affected by the following trends outlined by ACRL: ongoing budget challenges, the requirement that librarians possess diverse skill sets, the necessity of digitizing the unique collections found in libraries, and a mandate for increased collaboration both inside and outside the institution (ACRL Planning and Review Committee 2010).

The trends in arts libraries necessarily mirror the trends in general academic library settings because arts libraries are often part of academic libraries, whether the art library exists as a separate branch library or is a distinct collection within a larger academic library building. Each of the trends just outlined can be constituted as a challenge to the very mission of arts libraries, of which reference services are a core component.

Arts libraries play a specific role in the academic library enterprise because at the center of the arts library is the primacy of the image; visual materials exist at the heart of the art library reference services. In order to meet the challenges of an uncertain future, reference in arts libraries must focus on elements that differ from, yet complement, those offered by other library units. Each challenge outlined by ACRL is daunting, and only in collaboration with colleagues will each challenge be met. Yet each challenge can also be viewed through the lens of the skills of arts information professionals and the strengths of art library collections, with an eye toward the specific and unique contributions arts information professionals can bring to the reference encounter.

Budget Challenges

Budget "challenges" are now endemic and have evolved into a constantly looming threat to personnel, collections, and services. Resource costs increase annually, while funding for both collection development and personnel remains static or declines. Even if electronic databases in the arts, to name one format for resources, are significantly less expensive than their STEM (Science, Technology, Engineering, and Mathematics) counterparts, both database and art book costs remain an important consideration in any arts library budget. The arts remain book disciplines, and e-books supplement, but have yet to displace, their print counterparts in arts fields. This is likely because of a few main issues: the difficulties associated with electronic image quality, the challenges surrounding the reproduction in an electronic format of images that are subject to copyright and image permissions issues, and the importance of the traditional monograph to academic promotion and tenure in arts disciplines. It is likely that the arts will remain a book discipline for some time to come, and, therefore, book costs continue to be an important consideration in arts librarianship.

Diverse Skill Sets

For reference services in the arts library to continue to grow, arts information professionals will have to get out from behind the reference desk. This is both a literal and a figurative statement, and it is not a new idea. Embedded librarianship is one way to move beyond the physical confines of the reference desk. However, librarians have also been engaging with users in other ways that expand and extend the reference encounter. Librarians are teachers, and in many ways, the reference encounter is a search for the "teachable moment." Across the field, librarians have shifted the reference encounter from a focus on tools (recommending a particular resource) to a central focus on content and how to locate, evaluate, and employ sources. Reference encounters can variously translate into the construction of a library resource guide or web pathfinder, can lead to one-shot library instruction sessions, or can facilitate a dialogue with the professor of a particular course. Likewise, part of the reference transaction can be a search for opportunities to share information about the interdisciplinary uses of images. For arts information professionals, every reference encounter is an opportunity to educate about the image, both with patrons drawn from disciplines traditionally associated with the study of the image and with those students and faculty allied with departments in which the image is not at the center of study.

In discussing the role of imagery with patrons across the disciplines, arts information professionals are marshalling their diverse skill sets to advance information literacy efforts. In the future, reference in the arts will mean emphasizing visual literacy as part of a set of multiple literacies. Visual literacy is defined as "a set of abilities that enables an individual to effectively find, interpret, evaluate, use, and create images and visual media" (Hattwig et al. 2011, 1). Arts information professionals must continue to develop and share their own expertise in visual literacy. In the wake of recent reaccreditation studies, information literacy requirements, based largely on textual research, have been infused into a range of curricula, sometimes at the college level, and at other times at the departmental level. Many information professionals are familiar with the ACRL's (2000) "Information Literacy Competency Standards for Higher Education" (and other standards in the suite authored by ACRL), and they employ such standards as part of a formal information literacy program, as part of their personal instructional practice in the classroom, or in the context of working individually with students during a brief reference encounter or in more extended research consultations.

In 2006, the Art Libraries Society of North America (ARLIS/NA) published "Information Competencies for Students in Design Disciplines," a document intended to foster the information literacy of arts students and to allow for a discussion of the integration of teaching such skill sets into arts education and curricula (Brown et al. 2006). These competencies also advance general information literacy competencies for arts and design students while acknowledging and detailing the information literacy skill sets required in specific arts and design disciplines, differentiating those skill sets required by art history students, for example, from those crucial to fashion students. Later, Rockenbach and Fabian (2008) revisited the ACRL Information Literacy Competency Standards and framed them through the lens of visual literacy, noting that "visual literacy can be understood as a form of critical viewing just as information literacy can be understood as critical thinking" (29).

Rockenbach and Fabian's (2008) work marked an important attempt to bridge the textual and the visual in the professional practice of librarians in their work with students and faculty. Most recently, the ACRL issued "Visual Literacy Competency Standards for Higher Education," which situates information literacy in the higher education context and specifies six standards with performance indicators and learning outcomes for each standard (Hattwig et al. 2011). These are worthwhile efforts because in recent years disciplines outside of the arts have begun to use imagery in their research, not merely for illustrative purposes, but to analytical ends—in order to advance scholarly argument—as well. Such uses of imagery are appropriate in disciplines outside of the arts given how thoroughly today's students are immersed in visual culture. Using imagery is, quite simply, a way to relate to students. However, the familiarity of students with imagery may not necessarily equate with their possessing the tools to analyze and be critically engaged with the images they encounter, not only as part of their studies, but as part of their daily lives.

Digitizing Unique Collections

In recent years, there has been increased emphasis on "surfacing hidden collections" in an attempt to create minimal access points for those archival and special collections that had long lingered in backlogs. By making such collections "discoverable" by Internet search engines, the hope is to make them available to a wider range of researchers. It may then be possible to learn from use statistics and other measures which collections might merit more detailed processing and cataloging as well as enhanced digitization efforts (ARL 2009; Green and Meissner 2005).

Digitization reflects user expectations—those with whom arts information professionals work want to access all of the library's resources easily and completely. The expectation is for digitization and full-text access across *all* library resources. Ease of use and immediacy of access are at the forefront of patron needs. Users are clear in their expectations: "I want it all, and I want it right now." Faced with this demand, librarians must grapple with real concerns about digitization and preservation work flow and costs. Arts libraries must consider how they will participate in larger, organizational digital initiatives and argue for how the image resources held in art library collections might play a pivotal role in such projects. In all projects, issues surrounding accessibility remain a serious concern. There remains a digital divide, a barrier to *access* to technology that remains in place for many. Also, accessibility of the image for those with visual and other impairments is a significant challenge. Web content accessibility guidelines and the use of assistive technologies as necessary are helpful, but the size of online images is often limited due to copyright or other concerns. It is useful for arts information professionals to develop growing awareness of accessibility in their work with patrons. Indeed, in choosing pilot projects, consideration of audience is a major concern. Priority projects might appeal to an audience the institution most wants to serve, foster opportunities for curricular integration, open the use of imagery to a new group, or address long-standing institutional emphases.

Exposing hidden collections in this way reflects a growing understanding and acceptance of the ways arts library users increasingly find resources of interest to them, namely, through Google. Generally, such discussions of hidden collections refers to those items held in Special Collections—in other words, those resources held in restricted access and use environments. Arts libraries often have restricted use collections, but they may also have what can be termed "small s, small c" special collections; the use of the lowercase "s" and "c" serves as shorthand for collections that, while not rare nor financially valuable, may nonetheless be infrequently held or speak to areas of study that relate to institutional specialties or future initiatives.

These special collections can include objects and artifacts, primary sources, classic tomes by or about artists, artists' books, and a range of other resources. Such collections remain particularly useful in arts research, for a variety of reasons. First, in art historical study, a particular vein of scholarship may go out of vogue, but it does not go out of date. Thorough researchers are responsible for accounting for the entire bibliographic chain that connects the earliest scholarship on an artist, movement, or theme in the history of art to the most recent scholarship, paying special attention to the primary source material and the classic and seminal texts that link the earliest and most recent scholarship. The image is central to the arts; however, students may often have much more experience with the *reproduced* image (the digital surrogate) than with the actual object or artifact, whether print, painting, and so forth.

Increased Collaboration

Marketing what is unique, rare, seminal, or unusual in arts library collections in order to encourage use increases the value of library collections and marks a contribution of the library to the institution, to scholarship, and to the world of knowledge. Targeting specific classes and talking with professors and administrators about collections is a way of marketing available collections and services; outreach activities also drive reference transactions and consultations. Libraries are indeed creating reference opportunities by targeting classes for bibliographic instruction because such sessions often encourage students to pursue in-depth reference consultations.

The future of reference in arts libraries will rest in part on the ability of arts information professionals to collaborate effectively. Increased collaboration has been in part necessitated by a variety of forces, including reduced resources, emerging assessment mandates, and continually changing customer expectations. As in other disciplines, arts information professionals must be willing to collaborate with a wide range of potential partners. Collaboration within arts circles is expected; indeed, collaborative exchange is a key factor in creative endeavors, despite persistent myths about the solitary genius-artist. Collaboration between subject liaisons serving a range of subject disciplines will also remain important, as librarians seek to learn from one another and to foster inter- or cross-disciplinary research opportunities for their primary clientele. Collaboration between librarians and faculty members will remain of paramount importance. The field of librarianship has seen highly successful collaborative practices in a range of areas as librarians partner with academic faculty and administrative staff in order to engage students and advance student success (Raspa and Ward 2000; Swartz, Carlisle, and Uyeki 2007).

The challenge for arts librarians remains to forge unexpected partnerships in the institution, to reach out beyond traditional communities. Such strategies might involve telling "success" stories—about work with students, about the uniqueness of the collections—to any and all who will listen and, in return, listening to the stories of others. Such conversations may sow the seeds of collaboration that Raspa and Ward (2000), a librarian and a faculty member, write about in the *Collaborative Imperative*. The increasing proactivity of reference may help foster the movement from networking to coordination to the kind of rich collaboration Raspa and Ward advocate.

The Value of Art Libraries

Academic libraries are under pressure; these pressures—economic, social, and administrative—will likely increase in coming years. Libraries will continue to face significant resource constriction—will be expected to do more with less and will be faced with both declining budgets and enhanced patron expectations. Arts libraries may be particularly vulnerable. If the academic arts library is under threat, one reason is because the economic climate in higher education has led to questions about the value of the liberal arts to the academic enterprise. Arts libraries will be encouraged to demonstrate that they have a positive effect on what the university measures and cares about (ACRL 2010). At a recent Association of Research Libraries (ARL) Fall Forum, keynote speaker and Louisiana State University system President John Lombardi encouraged libraries and librarians to focus squarely on *what brings prestige* to the institution (Howard 2011).

Determining how best to assess the arts library's contribution to what the university values will likely require a variety of methodologies. There has been a range of formal programs to assess users' experience of the libraries and their services, including surveys, focus groups, user experience studies, and ethnographic studies. Making a case for the value of the arts library will require the strategic use of both quantitative and qualitative data. Part of assessing what works in libraries, what meets and exceeds patron expectations, involves, as a recent title pointedly tells us, *Listening to the Customer* (Hernon and Matthews 2011). In this book, Hernon and Matthews point out that the most rich communication method is one-to-one interaction. The reference encounter, whether via live chat, e-mail, or in person, is precisely the kind of one-to-one exchange that gives us the chance to informally ask patrons what is working or what is not working, not only about reference transactions and services, but also about the arts library more generally. The assessment mandate will continue to expand, and librarians will have to do more to demonstrate their value. ACRL's (2010) *Value of Academic Libraries* presents a broad vision to engage with such an effort and offers a challenge to information professionals. For the purposes of this chapter, reference services provide an ongoing opportunity to open conversations through which librarians might gather valuable input, as well as tell the library's story.

Conclusion

Despite the pressures on libraries, the changing nature of reference, and questions about the relevance and utility of our field, art librarians must engage in their professional practice with a spirit of optimism. If they do not, it is difficult to see how arts information professionals can connect with, respond to, and best serve patrons, especially students. Recent scholarship has posited that students may not want to forge a connection with librarians as part of the reference encounter (Kennedy 2011). In the future, reference may mean offering service to all, while focusing on self-selected patrons who request a person-to-person exchange in whatever format. The self-selected group requesting in-depth reference assistance may be working on advanced projects or might need additional guidance as they begin new research endeavors. For those others who desire an unmediated reference process, the challenge to librarians will lie in honoring the connection with the patron while getting out of his or her way.

At its core, the reference encounter in any format is about human exchange. The self-conscious creation of art is what marks our common humanity. Among the prehistoric cave paintings in Perle Meche (Lot, France), which date back to 25,000 BCE, is a striking image of a human hand. This image was created when someone placed their hand against the cave wall and blew red pigment over it. The resulting image, which has survived for thousands of years, is a mark of agency, a mark of presence, despite its long-absent creator. In working with patrons, even if our presence is increasingly invisible, the hand of the arts information professional can continue to positively guide and shape the reference enterprise.

REFERENCES

ACRL (Association of College and Research Libraries). 2000. "Information Literacy Competency Standards for Higher Education." American Library Association. Approved January 18. www.acrl.org/ala/mgrps/divs/acrl/standards/standards.pdf.

———. 2010. *The Value of Academic Libraries: A Comprehensive Research Review and Report.* Prepared by Megan Oakleaf. American Library Association. www.ala.org/acrl/sites/ala.org.acrl/files/content/issues/value/val_report.pdf.

ACRL Planning and Review Committee. 2010. "2010 Top Ten Trends in Academic Libraries: A Review of the Current Literature." *College and Research Libraries News* 71 (6): 286–92.

Applegate, Rachel. 2008. "Whose Decline? Which Academic Libraries Are 'Deserted' in Terms of Reference Transactions?" *Reference and User Services Quarterly* 48 (2): 176–89.

ARL (Association of Research Libraries). 2009. "Special Collections in ARL Libraries: A Discussion Report from the ARL Working Group on Special Collections." Association of Research Libraries. Published March. www.arl.org/bm~doc/scwg-report.pdf.

Arndt, Theresa S. 2010. "Reference Service without the Desk." *Reference Services Review* 38 (1): 71–80.

Brown, Jeanne, Jane Carlin, Thomas Caswell, Edith Crowe, Maya Gervits, Susan Lewis, Alan Michelson, Barbara Opar, and Jennifer Parker. 2006. "Information Competencies for Students in Design Disciplines." Art Libraries Society of North America. Updated with additions July 2007. www.arlisna.org/images/researchreports/informationcomp.pdf.

Carlson, Jake, and Ruth Kneale. 2011. "Embedded Librarianship in the Research Context: Navigating New Waters." *College and Research Libraries News* 72 (3): 167–70.

Cassel, Kay Ann. 2010. "Meeting Users' Needs through New Reference Service Models." In *Reference Renaissance: Current and Future Trends*, edited by Marie L. Radford and R. David Lankes, 153–60. New York: Neal-Schuman.

Greene, Mark A., and Dennis Meissner. 2005. "More Product, Less Process: Revamping Traditional Archival Processing." *The American Archivist* 68 (Fall/Winter): 208–63.

Hattwig, Denise, Joanna Burgess, Kaila Bussert, and Ann Medaille. 2011. "ACRL Visual Literacy Competency Standards for Higher Education." Association of College and Research Libraries. Approved October. www.ala.org/acrl/sites/ala.org.acrl/files/content/standards/visualliteracy.pdf.

Hernon, Peter, and Joseph R. Matthews. 2011. *Listening to the Customer.* Santa Barbara, CA: Libraries Unlimited.

Howard, Jennifer. 2011. "Research Librarians Consider the Risks and Rewards of Collaboration." *Chronicle of Higher Education*, October 16. http://chronicle.com/blogs/wiredcampus/research-librarians-consider-the-risks-and-rewards-of-collaboration/33694.

Kennedy, Scott. 2011. "Farewell to the Reference Librarian." *Journal of Library Administration* 51 (43): 319–25.

Kvenild, Cassandra, and Kaijsa Calkins, eds. 2011. *Embedded Librarians: Moving Beyond One-Shot Instruction.* Chicago: American Library Association.

Novotny, Eric, comp. 2002. *Reference Service Statistics and Assessment.* SPEC Kit 268. Washington, DC: Association of Research Libraries.

Radford, Marie L., and R. David Lankes, eds. 2010. *Reference Renaissance: Current and Future Trends.* New York: Neal-Schuman.

Raspa, Dick, and Dane Ward, eds. 2000. *The Collaborative Imperative: Librarians and Faculty Working Together in the Information Universe*. Chicago: American Library Association.

Rockenbach, Barbara, and Carole Ann Fabian. 2008. "Visual Literacy in the Age of Participation." *Art Documentation* 27 (2): 26–31.

Swartz, Pauline S., Brian A. Carlisle, and E. Chisato Uyeki. 2007. "Libraries and Student Affairs: Partners for Student Success." *Reference Services Review* 35 (1): 109–22.

Wilson, Terrie, ed. 2003. *The Twenty-First Century Art Librarian*. New York: Routledge.

Part III

"DUDE, WHERE'S MY JETPACK?"
Near Future of Reference

Whither Libraries?

User-Driven Changes in the Future of Reference

John Gibson

W ithout the aid of a DeLorean or the assistance of Michael J. Fox, this chapter goes back to the past to understand the present and to speculate on the future. It is of course impossible to know exactly what the makeup of tomorrow's library will be. However, using what is known about developing technologies, this chapter attempts to predict the course that libraries in general, and reference services in particular, will take in the years ahead, keeping firmly in mind this caveat: "Most stories set in the future are examinations of the present in glittery disguise" (Williams 2002, 79).

In 2002, this author presented at a conference at the University of Memphis; the topic was anonymous proxies and identity protection. At this conference, he began to develop a greater understanding of how innovation was a response to needs. The night before the conference, the attendees were given a brief tour of the improvements that the university was making in their classroom infrastructure. The tour guide noted several of the innovations that designers used in updating the campus. First, the floors were designed to handle high-speed fiber network connections. Second, the design of the classrooms exhibited a visually interesting use of space through its extension of the vertical lines of the rooms. One classroom in particular was exceptionally impressive; the layout of the new podium for this room was reminiscent of the Imperial Senate chamber in *Star Wars*. The acoustics were impeccable, and it was evident that much thought had been given to the needs of the faculty utilizing the space. Such attention to detail was evidence of how design elements were implemented in response to needs articulated by the students and faculty. Another example of this phenomenon of innovation in response to user need had to do with student computing. The Memphis students had requested quicker access to resources and more space in the classroom. Out of that need to improve available resources, there emerged state-of-the-art classrooms with high-end personal computers (PCs) and flexible floor plans to accommodate the students' needs. The University of Memphis is just one example of this kind of needs assessment, planning, and design implementation that holds promise for the future of students, faculty, and information professionals engaged in higher education. This discussion examines such changes in areas like storage, access, and creation of resources, and their impact on the library as possible precursors of the next evolutionary point.

Until very recently in the history of libraries, information was bound to a specific place (the library) and a specific set of materials (the collection) and access was constrained by limitations of time (the schedule of the physical place). A librarian mediated the access and retrieval experience. At the close of the twentieth century, due to innovations in information storage and retrieval brought about by the Internet and personal computing, those boundaries were broken. With the information revolution came new challenges. Patrons' information needs were, as they are now, the driving force for innovation. As libraries transitions from their brick-and-mortar past to their online future, assessment of and responses to the wants and needs of library patrons will be essential.

Reference and the Evolution of Technology

Historically libraries were envisioned as repositories of knowledge, dedicated to holding the thoughts and words of past generations. Until recently, due to limitations of space, librarians have often had to be selective about which resources would fill their buildings. Space restrictions were later offset by the age of the Internet, which provided new opportunities to store whole collections of data that would have been previously unthinkable. Reference librarians have made it their mission to teach patrons how to access and use digital resources (Woodward 2000). Librarianship, therefore, has appeared to take a new approach to dealing with change. Previously the library would expand local collections, but now many collections are globally accessible and easily shared. Some large collaborative projects have already helped to accelerate the transformation of the physical library. Examples include "the large digitization projects found in the Library of Congress's American Memory program, the Cooperative Digitization Project, the California Digital Library, the Cooperative Online Resource Catalog (CORC) initiated by OCLC and Journal Storage (JSTOR)" (Intner and Johnson 2008, 112). The library of tomorrow is evolving from a "collect and protect" mentality to the "search and share" mode. "To help meet the new collaboration needs of a digital society," libraries are responding in a number of ways, including offering distance education classrooms and teleconferencing centers (Woodward 2000, 121). The scope of change resulting from increased collaboration may someday prove to be the digital generation's Gutenberg press, as real information is being streamed from libraries and data centers into the homes of researchers. Julie M. Still's chapter in this book, "A History of Reference," provides an in-depth overview of the history of reference services. However, to put into focus the relationship between librarians and users, a brief historical discussion is in order.

Problems relating to the management of information and making it available to users are as old as written language. One of the first tasks of librarians was preservation of resources for both current and future scholars. During the Dark Ages in Europe, collective stores of knowledge were threatened by bands of marauding hordes. Scholars attempted to save that information from destruction by copying it, archiving it, and protecting it. (One could argue that this is somewhat analogous to how modern librarians rescue unique materials through the curatorship of special collections.) During that chaotic time, much of the written knowledge of humanity, as suggested in Cahill's (1995) *How the Irish Saved Civilization*, was forgotten or lost to fire and war:

> As the Roman Empire fell, as all through Europe matted, unwashed barbarians descended on the Roman cities, looting artifacts and burning books, the Irish, who were just learning to read and write, took up the great labor of copying all of western literature—everything they could lay their hands on. (3)

Cahill suggested that if not for the troves of data stored away in scrolls and harvested from ancient writing by scholars, later civilizations could have been in the dark for a long time.

During the Age of Enlightenment, as the world of knowledge burgeoned, librarians struggled to keep pace with user needs with regard to access and retrieval. One such response was the French cataloging code of 1791. Library scholar Judith Hopkins (1992) stated that this code "was notable for two reasons: it was the first national cataloging code and it was the first code to provide for the use of cards in the cataloging process, with playing cards serving as the medium of choice" (1). Thus, this inventory management system, the card catalog, was the solution to the user need for a method to track and categorize information about library books. At the beginning of the computer age in the late twentieth century, a solution was needed to assist researchers in retrieving great stores of data—data that had grown exponentially and was straining against the constraints of the physical card catalog system. During this time, librarians began to use digital indexes and digital catalog systems, which eventually became searchable on the Internet at many libraries.

The following scenario is typical of the current library reference experience. A library user stops at a reference desk, either in person or virtually, to ask for help for a variety of reasons (academic, personal, work related, etc.). After speaking with a reference librarian, the patron is able to access and utilize a selection of resources. If the user is not at the library, he or she may be accessing the librarian's expertise as well as the information using a PC or a mobile device. The user may access that data immediately, request that it be delivered in digital format, or request a physical artifact for delivery to the user's library of choice. This process is an evolution from previous models; in the past, library users would have to wait for the physical delivery of items in print that were not immediately available. It should also be noted that libraries are not only a storehouse of data, as they were in the past, but also a retrieval service. While the tools for finding, requesting, and retrieving information have changed, the mission of the reference librarian remains the same: to make information accessible and to instruct users in how to utilize it to meet their needs.

Amid radical changes in how information is stored, accessed, and retrieved, many societal factors remain. The new horizon offers challenges and unique opportunities for librarians to address the evolving state of the library. The next section looks at the current state of reference librarianship concerning the needs of information access by current users.

Current Challenges and Innovations

The reference librarians of today face challenges in information access ranging from digital rights management (DRM), artificial intelligence in smart
systems, and even the "deep web's" isolation of data (i.e., information that is
hidden out of reach of most search engines) to the problems associated with
utilizing tools and utilities that frequently change.

Legislation and Regulation

Perhaps one of the biggest issues facing librarianship today is the onslaught of
regulatory initiatives regarding the Internet, intellectual property, and DRM.

> DRM is commonly defined as the set of technological protection mea-
> sures (TPM) by which rights holders prevent the use of digital content
> they license in ways that could compromise the commercial value of
> their products. Restrictions on such uses as downloading, printing,
> saving and emailing content are encoded directly in the products or
> the hardware needed to use them and are therefore in immediate ef-
> fect. (Kasprowski 2010, 49)

Digital rights issues are divisive. Opponents of increased restrictions argue
that new technologies add new limitations that could be used to curtail the
creation and sharing of information. "The opponents argue that DRM is not
very effective in preventing piracy, but can prevent the legitimate users taking
full advantage of the digital media" (Rayna and Striukova 2008, 110). Rayna
and Striukova explained how DRM may make the acquisition of knowledge
difficult if not impossible in the future when historians need to access the
protected information. Proponents of the DRM movement argue that artists,
authors, and corporations need safeguards to protect digital assets and intellectual property that belong to them.

To help users to work within the constraints of DRM, librarians must educate themselves about the various regulations, including limitations with regard to copyright and fair use. Many librarians who take a stand in opposition
to DRM initiatives do so to prevent a future monopoly over intellectual content. There is also a concern about keeping information available to those users
who could be disenfranchised by the "digital divide." Information resources

(databases, subscriptions, etc.) are expensive. An unintended consequence of DRM regulations, taken to an extreme, is that they may create an information disparity between the "haves" and the "have-nots." This disparity may result not only due to economic factors (e.g., lack of a home PC and dependence on library computers) but also, as in the case of independent scholars, due to a lack of affiliation with a major research institution.

Artificial Intelligence

Libraries have many technologies at their disposal for delivering information and answering queries. "Smart response" artificial intelligence (AI) systems are being used to handle simple reference questions and requests. The Robeson Library at Rutgers University (www.libraries.rutgers.edu/robeson), for example, has a widget on its site called "Ask Gary." "Gary" is an automated "reference librarian" who answers reference questions via the Artificial Intelligence Markup Language (AIML). Essentially, "Gary" can respond to a basic request by "reading" and interpreting the context of a question and assessing it against a database of frequently asked questions. When no answer is possible, Gary will then help the patron reach live help via phone, chat, or e-mail.

Since 2011, AI systems have been integrated into Google's search function and into search products like Apple's Siri. With AI, the research is becoming more active, deep, and insightful. AI software development started to change significantly around 2011 with the development of the new programming language named Dart, a brainchild of Google, which represented a major "behind the scenes" innovation. The goal of the developers of these AI tools initially was to take routine facts and tasks and handle them via audio commands or, in some cases, via visual gestures (as in the Microsoft Xbox Kinect and Nintendo Wii entertainment systems). The implications of how these developments could change library reference, particularly library-user interface, are profound.

Libraries now have tools to help find online sources previously unavailable by using massive computing resources in the "cloud." The continued evolution of libraries will require both the user and information professional to have more familiarity with these tools; however, such mastery will enable the library user to spend more time in working on quality research and less time locating items buried deep inside databases that were often inaccessible. On the library side of the equation, library systems will need to invest in the supporting infrastructure and librarians will need to invest in the intellectual effort required for mastery of these tools. The technology will not remove the need for reference/research librarians but instead will utilize their analytical and teaching skills to enable users to be successful.

Crowd-Sourcing Information

The open source movement offers a nonproprietary and communal approach to the development of information resources and information tools; the movement advocates shared programming and information sharing. Data from storehouses like *Wikipedia* and operating systems like Linux has increased the amount of shared knowledge available. Creators of open source technologies have the mind-set that the greater collective will provide answers and resources that are more useful to more people, by harnessing the talents of many to focus on the same problems.

Wikipedia, the web-based encyclopedia, is a highly successful example of such a technique. Over time, the content of the articles is refined by input and fine-tuning by the masses of the resource's users and editors. *Wikipedia* has, of course, some drawbacks. The entries in *Wikipedia* are not intended to be primary resources in academia; from time to time, content is subject to "poisoning" by people with contrary opinions on a matter. However, this group-editing initiative has proven to be a highly successful and reasonable approach to information dissemination. The information in *Wikipedia* provides a useful starting point, particularly so with well-documented entries (i.e., those with citations and outside links). As with any encyclopedia article, however, information should be verified and supplemented with other sources, particularly so if one is writing a scholarly or professional paper.

Google, the Internet search engine powerhouse, has expanded. Critics have branded it as a major challenge to libraries because it has similar goals as libraries, including the reference/research function (Chad and Miller 2005, 5). By the simple act of entering a search term, a user taps into the power of Google Books, Google Scholar, Google Images, as well as the treasure trove of information accessible on the web. Recognizing this power and ease of use, reference librarians are also figuring out how to utilize Google, how to instruct patrons on its effective use, and how to develop partnerships with the corporation. For example, a person may be seeking information on the island of Java. A Google search will yield some geographical information, but most of the initial hits will be about the programming language used to develop software. A librarian who is competent in customizing research queries and knowledge-able about the workings of Google and its search algorithms will be able to guide users through more efficient use of the power of this search tool. The sheer number of hits can be overwhelming to a student or a novice researcher. The librarian can serve as a guide in teaching and promoting information lit-eracy skills: to steer these users to the correct tools (perhaps Google Scholar); to help the user create effective search queries; and to help the user verify the validity and/or the utility of the hits returned.

Technology

A number of technologies on the horizon will profoundly influence how in-formation is delivered. In turn, these technologies will profoundly influence the interaction of reference librarians and end users. As an example, near-field wireless (NFW) communications is a technology that allows small devices to communicate with each other. PayPal can utilize wireless technology to perform transactions on some mobile smart devices. Such technology could expand to libraries; it might be adapted for patron material transactions and identity confirmation. Libraries are now expanding videoconferencing to remotely help support patrons despite distance barriers. The idea is that pa-trons who are unable to make it into the library buildings can still have an effective and positive reference experience. Currently, similar technology is now being used to support chat and other communication avenues. It might be that such technology, when combined with new research tools, will some-day allow larger libraries to support satellite locations. As funding continues to decrease, many library systems will be challenged on how to meet growing demand for user services; new technologies may be able to provide greater efficiencies for offering system-wide information resources and services such as reference and instruction.

To meet the growing needs of the virtual library patron, librarians will likely turn even to communication resources available through the web. Social media can help people become more aware of changes and resources at librar-ies and can simultaneously reach a larger audience. One could argue that tools like Facebook and Twitter have made possible the ability to interact with pa-trons across the nation. The digital revolution continues to provide new tools for virtual communication. Technologies like QR (quick response) codes provide a sort of reality layer over virtual bookmarks—bar codes repurposed for a new generation. These bar codes allow businesses to extend their reach to customers anywhere they can envision a printable square. A QR code can contain metadata about a product that, when used with a reader, can help visualize resources on a computer or display screen. Libraries have adapted to social media sites, QR codes, and other technologies like self-scanning and self-checkout terminals, electronic book displays, and kiosks, and some have even created their own avatars, extending their digital assets by using the physical world's information in the virtual world.

Conclusion

"Everything in this universe is perpetually in a state of change" (Aitchison 2001, 3). As can be gleaned from the proceeding discussion, the future of librarianship is one that encompasses new rules, technologies, and techniques that could eradicate old stereotypes about what a library is and what librarians do. The evolutionary changes in what constitutes a "library" and how that library interacts with its users will occur by refining what works and discarding that which does not. If the layout of all the future could be revealed in an "Ask Gary" query or by a question to Apple's Siri, life would be transparent. Alas, there is not yet a crystal ball app for that.

REFERENCES

Aitchison, Jean. 2001. *Language Change: Progress or Decay?* New York: Cambridge University Press.

Cahill, Thomas. 1995. *How the Irish Saved Cvilization: The Untold Story of Ireland's Heroic Role from the Fall of Rome to the Rise of Medieval Europe.* New York: Anchor Books.

Chad, Ken, and Paul Miller. 2005. "Do Libraries Matter? The Rise of Library 2.0." White Paper. Birmingham, UK: Talis. www.capita-libraries.co.uk/downloads/white _papers/DoLibrariesMatter.pdf.

Hopkins, Judith. 1992. "The 1791 French Cataloging Code and the Origins of the Card Catalog." *Libraries and Culture* 27 (4): 378–404.

Intner, Sheila S., and Peggy Johnson. 2008. *Fundamentals of Technical Services Management.* Chicago: American Library Association.

Kasprowski, Rafal. 2010. "Perspectives on DRM: Between Digital Rights Management and Digital Restrictions Management." *Bulletin of the American Society for Information Science and Technology* 36 (3): 49–54.

Rayna, Thierry, and Ludmilla Striukova. 2008. "White Knight or Trojan Horse? The Consequences of Digital Rights Management for Consumers, Firms and Society." *Communications and Strategies* 1 (69): 109–26.

Williams, Sam. 2002. *Arguing A.I.* New York: Random House.

Woodward, Jeannette. 2000. *Countdown to a New Library: Managing the Building Project.* Chicago: American Library Association.

9

Future World
Strategic Challenges for Reference in the Coming Decade

Stephen Abram

Without a doubt, the environment for libraries has changed immeasurably over the past few decades. Changes in the technological, social, demographic, and funding environments have necessitated that library management review the fundamental strategies for delivering services—that reference be reinvented for the new millennium. For the past few decades, there has been a reinvention of the basic infrastructure of libraries. Library systems have moved to greater collaboration. Cloud computing has emerged, as have mobile computing, new devices, e-learning, and social software. Each of these has contributed to a fundamentally different and radically change-oriented ecology. Content format and acquisition have been changed forever by massive digitization and the availability of both public and private repositories and databases of content via various formats. The "book" has been reinvented and, indeed, so has the concept of a "learning experience."

The role of technological change as a significant disruptor, enabler, and provider of opportunity is clear. What is happening, in this decade, is the internalization of social, learning, communication, information, and collaboration technologies as central to reference strategies rather than as a mere infrastructure enhancement. The social web, tools of engagement, Web 2.0, collaboration tools, e-learning, and other tools have transformed library strategies forever, and they will continue to do so. The world wherein desktop personal computers (PCs) were the dominant venue for computing; print content, television, radio, and film were the prevailing mass media; and education was delivered predominantly through a classroom experience is a world that is gone forever. A hybrid, multimodal paradigm is emerging, and this represents a wonderful and exciting opportunity for reference and research work. The opportunity to interact with all end users at the point of need and learning is tantalizingly close. The integration of reference services into the lesson level of learning, into the lab level of research, and into the hands of every user through mobile devices is revolutionary. The real challenge is to position reference service providers as consultative experts and the go-to folks in the minds of the end user. This chapter outlines the top strategic responses to this challenge. The ultimate outcome of all of this change is unknown, but the direction and the initial steps outlined herein will be essential to framing the opportunity for success in library reference services as libraries progress through the coming decades.

The changes just outlined have created seven key opportunities for librarians to use in coordinating reference and service strategies in the coming decades. They fall into the following "buckets": evidence-based reference strategies; experience-based portals (aka "The New Commons"); "quality strategies"; transliteracy strategies; people-driven strategies; curriculum and research agenda; and services and programs. At first glance, this list seems to have very little to do with technology, mainly because this new era is one that relies on a "post-technology" strategy. Technology is being placed in its original and correct position, as an enabler, a tool, and not as a strategy in and of itself. Libraries are about discovery, creativity, invention, community, learning, and more. Technology plays a key role in making these wonderful outputs of society, citizens, and institutions, and libraries have an expanded range of opportunities as a result. However, in this new century, librarians need to recommit to the central role of library institutions—of providing a framework for progress for people through people. Libraries and librarians have been key components of past successes in information innovations; future successes will be grounded in the collections, structures, standards, and services offered to researchers by the same. Therefore, it is important for libraries to evolve in the right direction of this new century, to thrive and continue to have a positive and valuable impact on social, cultural, and industrial progress. The sections that follow examine each of these "buckets" in detail.

Evidence-Based Reference Strategies

Historically, reference strategies have been built on an opportunistic basis. Librarians have observed a need through their interactions with researchers, students, and other users and developed and tested new modes to address these needs. In recent years, this has changed radically for several reasons. In many cases, the majority of reference questions are now occurring in an unmediated fashion through virtual use of databases, websites, and e-learning environments. This means that the in-person users, those whom librarians see face-to-face, may not actually be a representative sample of the cohort of users libraries seek to serve. Therefore, in-person observations are inadequate to drive strategy for future change. Technology has fundamentally shifted the perception of users and changed their demand patterns. They expect answers in a real-time and comprehensive fashion aligned with their work paradigm and habits. Opportunities (via various software and services) exist to drive library strategies with data or information that is easy to collect, know, and analyze. Librarians can use the data to test assumptions about user behaviors and to see the overlaps and gaps between virtual and in-person users, demographic differences in use, and the major questions and research domains that comprise the top areas in which librarians and library resources are asked for assistance. User behavior is now more transparent for those who seek to understand it and how it is evolving.

Opportunities for data-driven decisions abound. Librarians and administrators now have access to a variety of inexpensive (easy to gather) data that has become more readily available over the past twenty years, such as website traffic analytics; integrated library system (ILS) search patterns including raw statistics, analytics, and deep data; geographical and global positioning system (GPS) data; search statements; customer satisfaction data (such as ForeSee); and normative data including census and national data sets. Each of these different categories of data provides librarians with an opportunity to track real user behavior and adjust strategies in response.

Website Traffic Analytics

At present, Google Analytics can be utilized by a library website for no charge. There are also professional analytical tools that can be added to a library's web presence or used at a low cost through institutional adoption at the university, college, or municipal level. Some sample questions for analysis by librarians regarding the use of their website include what sites were visited that led the user to the library; where the users are geographically (whether they are of the target community); what library pages are most popular (most visited) and which are the least utilized; and whether the majority of the page hits are from in-house or from a home or an office setting. Answers to questions such as these can be extremely useful to the library's strategic planning team and provide information that is critical knowledge to drive both virtual and in-person reference strategies.

ILS Search Patterns: Raw Statistics, Analytics, Deep Data

As never before, an ILS can provide rich data for assessing how the collection is being used. For example, interlibrary loan (ILL) and circulation data provide insight into what are the most underused or overused parts of the collection. Holds and material requests from other institutions reveal the strengths and weakness of a library's collection. Knowing how a collection relates to the reference questions being asked provides a key metric in establishing whether the needs of users are being met.

GPS: Geography and Reference

GPS technology provides interesting opportunities for use as an assessment tool by reference librarians. It can provide answers to questions about both from whom and from where queries originate. Google currently provides a means for mapping (on simple Google maps) the sources of database, catalog, and website hits. For public libraries, for instance, this can be accomplished in a number of ways. If the cardholders log in, their general geographic information can be established from their patron record via their ZIP or postal code or the area code of their phone number. If they do not log in, their access point can still be mapped based on the geographic location of their Internet protocol (IP) address. Such information can be useful for determining underserved user communities based on area demographics. Academic libraries can use

GPS tools for determining rates of on- or off-campus library use and peak use times. Again, such data provides information for decisions about platforms and time frames for delivering reference services.

Search Statements

Licensed databases themselves provide a resource for user behavior data. Most suppliers can offer statistics on usage, many in COUNTER (Counting Online Usage of Networked Electronic Resources) or SUSHI (Standardized Usage Statistics Harvesting Initiative) compliant modes. Such data can be very useful on a universal basis and give year-over-year growth and change information. One limitation is that the data offered is mostly of a quantitative and not qualitative nature. Many suppliers, like Gale, will deliver a series of privacy-protected search statements organized by database that are often useful particularly when exported into a spreadsheet. Some questions that can potentially be addressed by these statistics are these: Does the content of the search differ in any meaningful way from searches done onsite? What role do typos play in queries and can this be addressed through user instruction or through interface design? Do the researchers use other strategies and tools in adding to keyword searching, and, again, is this an issue to address through instruction? Are patrons utilizing federated searches when they are offered? Finally, are any clues being offered as to the effectiveness of bibliographic instruction (e.g., is there an increase in more sophisticated search strategies following an instruction initiative)?

ForeSee Customer Satisfaction Data

ForeSee is an example of a web-based user satisfaction assessment tool. By comparing the library experience with the experience of user expectations with business-to-business, government, retail, and business-to-consumer websites, librarians and administrators can ensure that services offered to patrons are on a par with or surpassing benchmarks set in the public forum. Recent national data compiled by Gale[1] using ForeSee reveals the following statistics regarding users of library databases on a national basis: 27 percent of users are under eighteen; 59 percent are female; 29 percent are college students; 5 percent are professors; 6 percent are teachers; 29 percent found the databases via the library website; 59 percent found what they were looking for on their first search; 72 percent trust library content more than Google, but 81 percent still use Google (Gale internal statistics; but see, e.g., Gale Cengage Learning 2010). At the very least, these statistics indicate that libraries should strategize for inserting appropriate content and services in an e-learning environment at the course and lesson level to meet patron expectation and use patterns.

Normative Data and Census and National Data Sets

Accurate benchmarking techniques mandate that librarians and administrators have accurate data about their institutions and the demographics of their users. The comparison of a library to its peer institution serves to establish whether it is keeping up with (or exceeding) peer standards in such categories as collection, programs, staffing, and so forth. Useful sources for such data include the Institute of Museum and Library Services (IMLS), the American Library Association (ALA), the Association of College and Research Libraries (ACRL), the National Center for Education Statistics (NCES), and the Association of Research Libraries (ARL), which all provide benchmarking data. With regard to the demographics of library users, the latest (2010) census represents a major opportunity for libraries to assess changes in user populations at the system, metropolitan area, state/province, branch, and national levels (U.S. Census Bureau 2010).

This section discussed tools for compiling evidence for data-driven decisions. The next section explores some of the strategies that reference departments can utilize for putting that data to work in planning for their future.

Experience-Based Portals: The New Commons

Libraries have been building a "commons" strategy for many years now. Broadly, many libraries started with banks of public access computers that can now be viewed, retrospectively, as a computer commons. This created a situation in which librarians learned to handle complicated technology environments wherein devices, software, connectivity, resources, and services intersected. These evolved into community reference or research commons or information commons as they became less about technical architecture and more about services and programs. In recent years, more advanced knowledge and learning commons aligned with institutional mandates and strategies that demonstrate clear added value to the entire organization have emerged. There has been great progress, although overall implementation continues to be spotty, the overall evenness of distribution is affected by different foci at different institutions, and financial issues limit the speed of achieving grander visions. As they say, the future is here, it is just not evenly distributed yet.

Portal strategies are nothing new. Consumer web portals have existed for many years. What is new is the application of portal strategies on a scalable basis to library reference strategy portfolios. There are three key areas that frame the portal opportunity in the trend toward "portalization" of library service portfolios. These are driven by the following considerations: the individual institution's strategic plan; the top question domains; and the determination of the library's key projects or opportunities for development or experimentation. A strategic plan that is aligned with the library's institution or host community is key to the successful implementation of portal-based services. To be successful and to garner support—both financial and political—it is essential that a library's strategic plan be aligned with its funding body's. This needs to be done in a written strategic plan that uses language consistent with the larger organization's goals and objectives and that avoids library jargon and technical terms.

Reference departments are in the "business" of answering questions. The categorization of those questions can give librarians and library administrators some important evidence regarding user needs and a library's ability to meet those needs. The reference departments in public libraries, for instance, are frequently called upon to answer in areas such as general health and wellness; personal financial literacy; retirement planning; and book clubs or summer reading programs. An assessment of the areas in which patrons are expressing interest is a first step in establishing whether the library has or can adequately guide the users to the resources that they need.

The real power of determining the "top questions" lies in the fact that such an assessment can focus attention, effort, and priorities on the resources and a portal that will have the most impact and is tied most directly to the needs of the users. The value to the library is that such an assessment makes quality service scalable and improves and standardizes the basis for overall program scalability and sustainability.

Quality Strategies

It is essential that, in the first decades of this century, reference services define a positioning in user and institutional strategies that addresses where they fit in the ecosystem of search and research. That fit must be measurably better than the competitor offerings from web services such as Google and Bing. Gone is the day when reference librarians can sit at a desk and await questions; neither can they sit and wait by the phone, e-mail inbox, or messaging system. Librarians must actively seek to have a positive impact and clearly articulate their value in the competitive context of consumer versus professional and mediated search.

"Search engines," such as Google, are pushing the boundaries of the term. In addition to the integration of products and services (such as Google Scholar, Google Books, and Google's web interface Chrome), the sheer number of hits returned combined with the variety of formats offered (graphics, audio, and streaming media files) underscores the need for librarians to reposition themselves in public perception. The issues of the consumer search engine and its nonalignment or misalignment with end-user goals, while clear to an information professional, need also to be made clear to the users themselves. Thus, there is a strong opportunity for repositioning the library as a filter based on user needs for high-quality information to underpin learning objectives and decision support. End users will require help to improve the quality of their questions and their search results as well as guidance as to which resources will provide the optimum results. This trend is supported by four key foundations: the consumer search business model and search result pollution through search engine optimization and content spam factories; the continuing need for hybrid strategies of print and digital content; the ambiguous nature of quality in context; and the continuing need for human intervention to improve the quality of questions.

For the most part, questions that require the retrieval of facts (who, what, where, and when questions) are best accomplished via algorithmic-based search engines. The more difficult questions, those that require the juxtaposition or critiquing of ideas—the "hows" and the "whys," require the users to immerse themselves in a domain of knowledge and to discover answers by using specialized techniques and filters. Services like Google and Bing will continue to answer thousands of times more questions every hour than librarians can possibly hope to accomplish. However, complex questions, the important questions of decision support, learning, and support for careful, critical thinking, are where librarians can focus and shine in this era.

The consumer search model, as currently represented by Google, Bing, and Yahoo!, is based on a profit-producing model. Google can clear profits of up to $2 billion a month (U.S. Securities and Exchange Commission 2013). These for-profit search spaces have been criticized for manipulating results based on advertising and for collecting data on users for marketing purposes. Companies such as Google have responded by introducing updates to their algorithms (called Panda or Farmer) that attempt to ensure that some of the most egregious examples of manipulated content are balanced in the search results with some fairer, possibly higher-quality content. This has proven difficult to accomplish, given that the company itself depends on the same algorithm to deliver ads and sponsored links and the ecosystem of content farms and SEO (search engine optimization) professionals reacts quickly to adapt to any changes in the search algorithm.

Thus, the primary goal of the consumer search engine is to serve up groups of users to the paying customer—the advertising agencies and ad networks that pay the bills. The user is not the search engine's customer; the user is its product. This is a key differentiator between libraries and consumer search engines. Licensed databases and OPACs (online public access catalogs) in libraries or on library websites are never open to influence by advertisers or commercial or special interests. Unlike consumer search results, library searches would never be open to Holocaust deniers, white supremacists, politicians, or companies simply wanting to provide biased content about their products to assist searchers in their buying decisions. For libraries, the end user is always the focus. This fundamental difference is what reference librarians need to position in the minds of the public—the researchers, students, professionals, decision makers, and financers—that the central role of the libraries is to direct, select, and train the user in "quality" strategies and also to recognize "quality" in the information resources retrieved for essential tasks and important issues. The amorphous nature of that "quality" necessitates skilled human intervention. The value of the reference librarian's skill is embedded in the professional nature of question improvement strategies that are part of the library reference experience, whether in person or online.

Transliteracy Strategies

The meaning of "bibliographic instruction," and even "information literacy," has dramatically changed since the start of this new century. New paradigms, such as "transliteracy," are emerging (Ipri 2010). Transliteracy incorporates moving beyond the traditional concept of reading literacy and the more recent concept of information literacy to taking a wider approach. It addresses the key skills that are needed to be a functioning adult in the twenty-first century. In addition to basic literacy and information literacy, these skills include, but are not limited to, proficiency in numeracy; critical thinking and evaluation; finances; the analysis of media; and reputation, privacy, safety, and identity management. Librarians, teachers, and other information professionals can and should play a key role in this new multiliteracy required for a digital world. Indeed, the world of literacy has moved beyond computer, search, and reading literacy and now encompasses the very nature of human social interactions in which communication, sharing, creativity, discovery, and learning occur. By preparing students and all people for the challenges of living in the hybrid digital worlds of information and other social, learning, and community spaces, we can empower our users to achieve great success.

People-Driven Strategies

The world of consumer reference is primarily one of brand and is driven by brand loyalty strategies. This is clear just by listening to people talk about "Googling" something or "Facebooking" a friend. Libraries and librarians have a "brand" as well. As mentioned earlier, this brand is at once very strong and marked by trust, authenticity, and quality but also carries some worrisome traits, like slowness, nostalgically book bound, old-fashioned, and being more difficult and freighted with unfriendly policies (e.g., rules and fines). Social media are an effective tool for promoting the talents and expertise of the modern information professional as the best differentiator from consumer search engines and algorithmic search. By maintaining a professional presence on social media such as Facebook and Twitter, librarians can position themselves, their individual talents and expertise, to reach a new generation of potential library users. To date, the consumer search reference services have low brand recognition as personal search service providers. Despite the early business star power of Tom Anderson at MySpace, Steve Jobs at Apple, Bill Gates at Microsoft, Chad Hurley at YouTube, Sergey Brin or Larry Page at Google, Mark Zuckerberg at Facebook, Jack Dorsey at Twitter, or David Filo or Jerry Yang at Yahoo!, none of that translates into a personal connection. For this new century of reference librarianship, this rebranding of library professionals as information experts is a key opportunity for driving success. The evolution of social networks like Facebook, MySpace, Google+, Twitter, Yammer, Quora, blogs, and public or private social groups (Yammer, Ning, etc.) allow libraries to quickly and inexpensively reposition the talents of their people as relationships with users and align their professional talents to users based on a foundation of excellent and unique services and collections, both digital and print.

Curriculum and Research Agenda

The main host institutions, mostly educational and research driven, that employ reference librarians are stressed due to changes in the financial models that support these organizations. Everyone is being asked to justify their position and their role in the enterprise and the value they deliver. It is incumbent on library leaders to make the case for the positive impact of library operations on the success of the overall organization's mission. This requires strategic planning in order to articulate the value and alignment of the library to the whole institution's long-term success—in terms of people, technology, programs, operations, and collections. There is no longer a solid "public good" argument or "motherhood and apple pie" philosophy to fall back on. All libraries have to justify their existence in times of financial stress and new competitive threats from the vortex of innovation created by both public and private digital and web initiatives.

This state of affairs applies equally to librarians and libraries in K–12 schools, academic libraries in university and college settings, research support departments in public and business institutes, and special libraries that must align with business and organizational strategies. A number of professional return-on-investment and value studies published in recent years help in this direction. A fairly complete list of hundreds of studies is kept up-to-date at *Stephen's Lighthouse* (Abram 2013). There is also the tried-and-true strategy of collecting user stories and testimonials. The strategy needs to be to get all staff to communicate user value effectively and to engage users and key decision makers in the process of promoting the role of libraries and librarians. These strategies must be explicit and planned, and not just opportunistic.

Services and Programs

The role of reference workers and research support staff is becoming more important, rather than less. There are no scenarios in which individual collections will be sufficient to sustain a library's value and position in the organization. The process of digitization and increased access is continuing inexorably. The ability to link and search all or most repositories and e-book, e-article, and media collections is transformational and disruptive. Basically, reference services is moving to a place where access trumps collections, and individual filtering and evaluation skills have value in that environment. The role of the information professional has the opportunity to increase in value and status as a profession and professional partner. The trick will be energizing the profession as well as implementing institutional strategies to reposition the role of the librarian in the context of the overall institution, as opposed to allowing the library and the collection as a foundation to dominate strategic thinking. Therefore, strategies will be best positioned when they focus on people and needs and address the creation of sustainable, repeatable, and scalable programs that meet the needs of learners, researchers, and enterprises. The era of hand-knitting every reference question is well and truly over. This millennium will see the building of collaborative portals that address the key needs of users, and specialized reference work that is face-to-face will be reserved for high-impact populations of users.

This is the end game of the changes wrought by the new and emerging technologies and the new context of social institutions. Finally, libraries need a strategy that positions services and programs ahead of technology, collections, and metadata foundations but one that is fundamentally rooted in the history and success of libraries and their strengths in metadata, organization, access management, and description. Programs that involve the emerging strategies around embedded librarianship, advanced digital literacy librarians, experience design librarians, e-learning collaborations, and reference work by walking around—anything that involves the nexus of end-user needs and the coaching or transfer of skills to end users—will be the successful ones that propel reference services forward in this new century.

Conclusion

The time has come to take reference work to the next plateau, just as cataloging, acquisitions, systems, and management before it have evolved to more scalable strategies. Librarians and administrators must build on established successes in adapting to change in the past few decades and move beyond that *adaptation* to *transformation*. It is time to reimagine reference for a new era.

NOTE

1. Mr. Abram was Vice President of Cengage Learning (Gale).

REFERENCES

Abram, Stephen. 2013. "Value of Libraries Megapost." *Stephen's Lighthouse* (blog), August 29. http://stephenslighthouse.com/2013/08/29/value-of-libraries-megapost.

Gale Cengage Learning. 2010. "iCONN User Satisfaction Summary—August 2009 to December 2010." www.iconn.org/documents/iCONN_User_Satisfaction_Survey-minus_Gale_Comparison.pdf.

Ipri, Tom. 2010. "Introducing Transliteracy." *College and Research Libraries News* 71 (10): 532–67.

U.S. Census Bureau. 2010. "United States Census 2010." http://census.gov/2010census.

U.S. Securities and Exchange Commission. 2013. "Form 10-K: Google Inc." http://investor.google.com/pdf/20131231_google_10K.pdf.

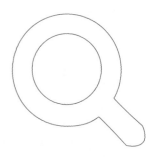

LibraryNext: Reference in 2052

John Gibson

Welcome to the library of the mid-twenty-first century. The "library" has evolved in some radical ways since the beginning of the century. It is much more connected to its resources; it is a marvel of technology. Libraries utilize equipment with self-powered screens that are impervious to destruction. Contents are displayed on these screens via touch-based interfaces with neural interconnects. New technologies have opened up new avenues of research in the library for those without systems at home (although lack of home access is now increasingly rare since computing devices are cheap and ubiquitous). Libraries provide virtual spaces where individuals and groups can meet through holograms or avatars. Privacy is preserved using acoustic dampers. Free online training programs from universities like MIT have continued to expand to include individuals who could not afford training and have evolved into transcontinental phenomena of academic support across the economic digital divide.

In the early millennium library, patrons typed their papers on QWERTY keyboards. They proofread their products by using primitive spell-checking software. During that era, scholars submitted their work for peer review prior to publication to determine their scholarly status. Now papers "self-heal" from errors, grammar is changed automatically, and individuals are able to utilize the "I am feeling lucky" filter on their research to have the results formatted properly in specific styles of documentation. Peer review is done collaboratively via wikis on the web. Access and use of images has also been vastly improved. Google's Picasa image editor allows users to perform a single-step fix for poorly exposed photos. Seamlessly integrated research and editing tools now allow scholars of all levels to produce correctly formatted, properly cited papers and collaboratively edited works.

The acts of research and writing have been revolutionized. Individuals can simply think ideas and then popular resources are made available to them both visually and audibly via their computing devices. In this projected future, "The planet has been Googled" (Auletta 2009, 282). Technology once used to help wounded soldiers operate prosthetic limbs or interact with computer systems via brain waves has been refined, introduced into the commercial market, and sold to the public. Data retrieval, once seen as a form of searching for information, is now a faster and more refined intuitive process done via thought in many cases. With the use of special neurotransmitters, a query to a virtual GPS (global positioning system) unit or search engine is now visually and electronically evident to the user via an apparatus of integrated information or as visible public displays. The hologram interface that people use to control their smart devices essentially derives from early technologies like those seen in the CNN election coverage of 2008 using 360BrandVision (Vilardell 2008).

Users are now directly connected to the services that they need instantaneously and on demand. Librarians have instant access to most data collections worldwide. The public demanded information freedom in much the same way that they demanded political freedom in the past. One of the first times this yearning for freedom was observed was during the original SOPA (Stop Online Piracy Act) and PIPA (PROTECT IP Act; Preventing Real Online Threats to Economic Creativity and Theft of Intellectual Property Act) laws of 2012, a time when the legislative branch of the government tried to enact expanded powers over the Internet. It was then that the public stood up with several corporations in a democratic process to convince the government that the preservation of the open Internet was a vital goal to the people (Lee 2012). During this era, it was recognized that information is power and that society needs to have both free and fair access. Librarians are no longer restricted to small data sets; they can help patrons instantly and with ease. Groups of trainers are available to add to assisted artificial intelligence (AI) interfaces that field generic questions that do not require emotional evaluation or untested theories.

Wireless is now free universally and its speed is now adaptive to the needs of the research. In the past, everyone was given "pipeline access" for sending and receiving data. The "pipe" was essentially a fixed size and would limit people based on their Internet service provider (ISP) setup and monthly payment plan. Now everyone shares equally and proportionally the amount of available bandwidth. Data determines packet traversal of information on the Internet. In the past, similar services existed, such as quality-of-service streams, which could prioritize packets for things like video communications, but now there is a much more intelligent system in place. An artificial packet agent for security and efficiency now maintains each stream. These agents efficiently handle and service the needs of the people, with or without inspection of the actual data. Services now connect at speeds that are fast enough that the end users are considered the biggest bottlenecks.

Learning is no longer limited by physical space; information is available wherever a person may travel. Quality, real-time translations for any known language are available as audio downloads, as are adaptive technologies for users with special needs via audio harmonizers and neurotransmitters. This allows information to be conveyed easily and helps bypass usability barriers. Available brick-and-mortar space is still used by libraries for archival and collaborative needs, and "despite a shift to more electronic usage of library resources, physical space is still an important factor in perceptions of resources" (Gerke and Maness 2010, 27).

In 2011, Hewlett-Packard briefly attempted to scuttle many of its hardware devices, perhaps prematurely, to make way for a digital future. The maker announced that they were also releasing memristors, a technology with advanced properties for handling data signals (Hewlett-Packard Development Company 2011). Memristors made it so that storage speeds and memory would accelerate radically. This upgrade allowed services that had web-only applications to be transferred to very small devices and be able to access large data sets. The first obvious application of this technology, through software, was the development of an application called LHsee. LHsee was created for the Android operating system by a group at Oxford University (Wilton 2011). LHsee allowed anyone in the world to connect to the LHC (Large Hadron Collider), the particle accelerator through which scientists are studying the universe.

In the early part of the twenty-first century, machines were being developed to compete with humans on game shows like *Jeopardy!* and be able to process real questions in context (Baker 2011, 1). It should be noted that AI during this era was a concern to some. There were people who envisioned a postapocalyptic world run by machines. Even with reservations, some must have thought that the world could not continue to grow profitably without the adoption of technological interfaces. AI systems became popularized through products like Apple's Siri. Research via AI, "smart" engines that could learn, became deep and insightful. Software development started to change significantly around 2011 with the development of the new programming language named Dart, a brainchild of Google. It was used behind the scenes in future developments. All the while computer labs around campuses across the United States evolved even more.

During this era, libraries of all stripes reached the conclusion that large print collections were neither sustainable nor necessary. As one scholar of the era noted, "Signals pointed to the demise of the print collection for some time" (Garrison 2011, 14). The question arose about how best to handle archival materials for future scholars. Resources available on the Internet became even more attractive as funding for libraries became more and more limited. Cooperative archiving strategies and enabling legislation with regard to copyright clearance paved the wave for large-scale digitization efforts. During the first decades of the twenty-first century, libraries reinvented themselves. Some facilities became study locations for peer mentoring and resource training; some just merged into the larger libraries around them (Thibodeau 2010). Physical collections still existed for unique and rare materials, such as first editions or historically significant works.

Although initially plagued with trepidation, citizens, librarians, and library administrators embraced a new path for libraries and library services as one full of optimistic changes and possibilities. The "library" is now free of many of the constraints evident from the previous era, such as the prohibitive digital rights management regulations and network congestion. Legislation, both domestically and internationally, determined that much of the information had to become available to all.

Society realized again that the freedom of the people was dependent on the freedom of speech. Library services, including reference services, were liberated, able to operate making full use of the intellectual material available on the World Wide Web.

REFERENCES

Auletta, Ken. 2009. *Googled: The End of the World as We Know It.* New York: Penguin.

Baker, Stephen. 2011. *Final Jeopardy.* New York: Houghton Mifflin Harcourt.

Garrison, Julie. 2011. "What Do We Do Now? A Case for Abandoning Yesterday and Making the Future." *References and User Services Quarterly* 51 (1): 12–14.

Gerke, Jennifer, and Jack M. Maness. 2010. "The Physical and the Virtual: The Relationship between Library as Place and Electronic Collections." *College and Research Libraries* 71 (1): 20–31.

Hewlett-Packard Development Company. 2011. "Revealed: The Material Properties of Memristors." Posted May 16. www.hpl.hp.com/news/2011/apr-jun/memristors.html.

Lee, Timothy B. 2012. "Internet Wins: SOPA and PIPA Both Shelved." *Ars Technica,* January 20. http://arstechnica.com/tech-policy/news/2012/01/internet-wins -sopa-and-pipa-both-shelved.ars.

Thibodeau, Patricia L. 2010. "When the Library Is Located in Prime Real Estate: A Case Study on the Loss of Space from the Duke University Medical Center Library and Archives." *Journal of the Medical Library Association* 98 (1): 25–28.

Vilardell, Nick. 2008. "Newest Technology: 360Brandvision™ Offers 3D Video Holograms in 360 Degrees." *PRWeb.com,* November 10. www.prweb.com/releases/hologram/ technology/prweb1587394.htm.

Wilton, Pete. 2011. "App Puts LHC on Your Mobile." *Oxford Science Blog,* October 7. www.ox.ac.uk/media/science_blog/111007.html.

ABOUT THE EDITORS
AND CONTRIBUTORS

KATIE ELSON ANDERSON is a reference and instruction librarian at Paul Robeson Library, Rutgers University. She has edited and contributed to scholarly works on topics that include plagiarism, social media and society, popular culture and libraries, and children and YouTube.

VIBIANA BOWMAN CVETKOVIC is a reference librarian and the head of Access and Collection Services at the Paul Robeson Library, Rutgers University. She has edited scholarly press books and authored peer-reviewed articles on the topics of intellectual honesty and children's visual culture. Ms. Cvetkovic is a PhD candidate in the Childhood Studies program at Rutgers University, Camden, New Jersey.

STEPHEN ABRAM, MLS, a strategy and direction planning consultant for libraries and the information industry, is principal of Lighthouse Partners. He is also executive director of the Federation of Ontario Public Libraries. He is a library trend watcher, keynote speaker, innovator, and author of *Stephen's Lighthouse* blog. He has held executive leadership positions in libraries and at Cengage Learning (Gale), SirsiDynix, Thomson, ProQuest, and IHS.

SUSAN J. BECK is happily retired and splits her time living at the beach in Lewes, Delaware, and Naples, Florida. She worked as a university reference librarian for thirty-two years at Rutgers, the State University of New Jersey; the University of Alabama; and the Center for the Study of Ethnic Publications at Kent State University. She also taught in the library school education programs at both Rutgers and Alabama. She was professionally active in the American Library Association, serving as president of the Reference and User Services Association (RUSA) and chair of RUSA's Reference Services Section.

LAWRENCE V. GHEZZI joined the South Amboy School District in September 1996. In 2002, he accepted the position of the South Amboy Middle/High School Media Specialist. In addition to a degree in social science and a degree in liberal arts, he has a master's degree in educational media specialization, holds a New Jersey teaching certification for grades K–8, a New Jersey supervisor certification for grades K–12, and a New Jersey associate school library media specialist certification with advanced standing. Since 1996, he has been a certified member of the Literacy Volunteers of America.

JOHN GIBSON is an instructional technology specialist at Rutgers University with over a decade of experience in programming and development in higher education. John received awards in innovative technology and had several opportunities to present at local, state, and national levels on topics about technology and ethics. John also has had his works published in several books, professional journals, and newsletters.

GARY GOLDEN received his MS in librarianship from the University of Kentucky in 1974 and his PhD in library and information science from the University of Illinois in 1983. He has worked in public services and administration in academic research libraries over a forty-year career. He is currently the director of the Paul Robeson Library at Rutgers, the State University of New Jersey. Dr. Golden has presented his research at various national and international venues, has published in refereed journals, and has consulted for several academic libraries.

SARA HARRINGTON is the head of arts and archives for the Ohio University. Dr. Harrington received her PhD in art history, her MA in art history, and her ML all from Rutgers, the State University of New Jersey. She received her BA in art history and French from Boston College. She has an extensive scholarly publication record.

JUSTIN HOENKE is a teen librarian and video gaming enthusiast who has written about these subjects for publications such as *Library Journal* and *Voices of Youth Advocates* and is a regular contributor for the blog *Tame the Web*. Justin is a member of the 2010 American Library Association Emerging Leaders class and was named a *Library Journal* Mover & Shaker in March 2013. Justin is currently the coordinator of teen services at the Chattanooga Public Library in Chattanooga, Tennessee. Follow Justin on Twitter at @justinlibrarian and read his blog at www.justinthelibrarian.com.

WALTER JOHNSON is a public information assistant at the Middletown Township Public Library, Middletown, New Jersey. His job includes the design of program promotional posters, creation of weekly e-mails for program updates, photographing of program activities, and participation in marketing planning meetings.

JULIE M. STILL is part of the library faculty at the Paul Robeson Library on the Camden campus of Rutgers University. She has an MA in history from the University of Richmond and an MA in library science and a BA in history from the University of Missouri. She has presented and published on a variety of topics in library science and history. As a reference librarian, she has a particular interest in the history of reference.

ZARA WILKINSON is a reference librarian at the Camden campus of Rutgers University. She received her MLIS from the University of Pittsburgh in 2010 and has also earned a BA in English literature from the University of Pittsburgh and an MA in English literature from West Chester University. At Rutgers Camden, she is liaison to the departments of English, Fine Arts, Philosophy, and Religion and also participates in campus outreach activities.

INDEX